MINDS, BRAINS, AND PEOPLE

MINDS, BRAINS AND PEOPLE

BY

T. E. WILKERSON

CLARENDON PRESS · OXFORD

1974

Oxford University Press, Ely House, London W.1

GLASGOW   NEW YORK   TORONTO   MELBOURNE   WELLINGTON
CAPE TOWN   IBADAN   NAIROBI   DAR ES SALAAM   LUSAKA   ADDIS ABABA
DELHI   BOMBAY   CALCUTTA   MADRAS   KARACHI   LAHORE   DACCA
KUALA LUMPUR   SINGAPORE   HONG KONG   TOKYO

ISBN 0 19 824510 6

PRINTED IN GREAT BRITAIN BY
BUTLER & TANNER LTD,
FROME AND LONDON

FOREWORD

I hope no apology is required for attempting to write a book on various modern physicalist accounts of persons. It cannot be denied that the approach I have chosen is a trifle ambitious. Indeed some might say that my concentrating on rather general comparisons and contrasts between a traditional and a modern physicalist account of persons may generate rather than dispel confusion. But in reading the recent literature on physicalism I have felt there has been an excessive concentration on difficulties of detail in the work of Smart, Armstrong, and others. We have tended to lose sight of a more general and more important question, namely whether a physicalist account of persons is *in principle* preferable to a more traditional account, however difficult it may be to work out in detail. Although I have been concerned with some of the details, my main purpose has been to focus attention on that general problem. I would not claim that the arguments I have used are particularly original or the conclusions particularly conclusive. The debate is of course very much with us, and a number of interesting books and papers appeared after the book was substantially complete. They have therefore in many cases not been acknowledged.

My thanks are due to Mrs. Rita Lee, who typed so beautifully; to Professor Ryle, who saved me from numerous infelicities of style, and who convinced me that colons should usually, and commas can frequently, be avoided; and especially to Professor Antony Flew, who has given me considerable help and encouragement, both in this and in other matters.

Finally a note about footnotes: in an attempt to confine them within decent limits I have included only the titles of articles or books under discussion. Complete references will be found in the bibliography.

Nottingham, 1973.

CONTENTS

PART I

TWO KINDS OF METAPHYSICS

'Well, it takes all kinds', Miss Docker said. 'Personally, I like a good discussion, amongst friends, on a metaphysical theme.'

(Patrick White, 'A Cheery Soul', in *The Burnt Ones*.)

I

TWO KINDS OF METAPHYSICS

1. *Metaphysics*

IN the *Blue Book* Wittgenstein sets out very clearly what he takes to be the principles of philosophical inquiry:

> Philosophers constantly see the method of science before their eyes, and are irresistibly tempted to ask and answer questions in the way science does. This tendency is the real source of metaphysics, and leads the philosopher into complete darkness. I want to say here that it can never be our job to reduce anything to anything, or to explain anything. Philosophy really *is* 'purely descriptive'.[1]

And in the *Investigations* he adds: 'Philosophy simply puts everything before us, and neither explains nor deduces anything. . . . It is not our aim to refine or complete the system of rules for the use of our words in unheard-of ways.'[2] There are at least three connected doctrines to be extracted from his remarks: first, that the method of philosophy is essentially *a priori*, the method of science essentially empirical; second, that the *a priori* philosophical method is descriptive, and does not consist, even in part, in suggesting changes in the system of linguistic rules described; and third, in particular, the philosophical method does not consist, even in part, in trying to make the system of linguistic rules fit or reflect the results of science.

This may seem to many an excessively austere view of philosophical inquiry. A contrary view, the view that our scientific— and mathematical—interests may and should legitimately influence the direction of our philosophical thought, can be found in Quine's *Word and Object*:

> . . . a canonical idiom can be abstracted and then adhered to in the statement of one's scientific theory. The doctrine is that all traits of reality worthy of the name can be set down in an idiom of this austere

---

[1] L. Wittgenstein, *Blue and Brown Books*, p. 18.
[2] Id., *Philosophical Investigations*, Pt. I, §§ 126, 133.

form if in any idiom . . . It delimits what counts as scientifically admissible construction, and declares that whatever is not thus constructible from given terms must either be conceded the status of one more irreducibly given term or eschewed. The doctrine is philosophical in its breadth, however continuous with science in its motivation.[3]

If the rest of the book is to be taken as an example of the method at work, philosophical views may well reflect, or be designed to be compatible with, mathematics or science; the distinction between *a priori* and *a posteriori* reasoning may well collapse, leaving philosophy continuous with science.

Quine's method is a paradigm example of what Strawson has called revisionary metaphysics, just as Wittgenstein's is a paradigm example of descriptive metaphysics: 'Descriptive metaphysics is content to describe the actual structure of our thought about the world, revisionary metaphysics is concerned to produce a better structure.'[4] The general outline of the suggestion seems intuitively obvious. It is the task of the descriptive metaphysician to describe the general features of, and relations between, the concepts we employ in describing various individuals in the universe of discourse; it is the task of the revisionary metaphysician to propose certain changes in our stock of concepts. One does the annual stock-taking; the other suggests new brands.

Obvious qualifications spring to mind. First, not all revisionary metaphysicians are inspired by an interest in science or concerned to bolster their arguments by appealing to *a posteriori* truths. Berkeley revised our stock of concepts more to glorify God than to glorify science (although he would probably have thought of himself as a descriptivist). And modern sense-datum theorists have been more interested in clarifying the language of perception than in recording advances in the physiology of perception; indeed excessive concentration on sense-data has probably hindered scientists by encouraging them to look for things that weren't there. Berkeleians and sense-datum theorists alike produced *a priori* arguments to support their conclusions. (The *Principles* in particular is full of invitations to reflect on a 'manifest repugnancy' in the notion of material substance, unsensed qualities, and so on.) However, having made that qualification, it is only realistic (remembering the subject of this book) to concede that many important revision-

3 W. V. O. Quine, *Word and Object*, pp. 228–9.
4 P. F. Strawson, *Individuals*, p. 9.

ary metaphysicians in this century *have* been inspired by science. We shall be concerned with the views of some of them.

There is a second qualification of the rather simple account of the distinction between descriptive and revisionary metaphysics. The descriptive metaphysician, I said, is concerned to describe the general features of, and relations between, the concepts we employ in the universe of discourse; the revisionary metaphysician proposes changes. But the expression 'individuals in the universe of discourse' is somewhat tricky. For the number and types of individuals are themselves functions (at least in part) of the concepts we employ. Although the actual structure of the world (whatever it may be) may place very broad restrictions on the sorts of things we can coherently say about it, there are numerous possible ways of mapping out the universe; there are numerous sets of individuals which may in turn be substituted for 'shoes, and ships and sealing-wax, and cabbages and kings . . .' The structure of the world places restrictions on the enterprise, in so far as we cannot introduce a distinction between two kinds of thing unless one kind is identifiably different from the other; nor indeed can we overlook differences between radically different kinds of thing (e.g. between things which burn us and those which do not). But within such limits we have a quite extensive choice in mapping out the universe of discourse. I can for example talk of a glass of water or of a collection of H_2O molecules or of a group of interacting particles or of a spatio-temporal water-slice or of a bit of Waterness or of a sensible partaker of Water Itself, and so on. The task of the metaphysician may be regarded at least in part as ontological. The descriptivist describes, in general terms, the kinds of individual we distinguish; the revisionary metaphysician makes proposals as to which kinds of individual *ought* to be distinguished.

To draw the distinction in this way may indeed seem reasonable and uncontroversial; controversy may appear only to arise when we go on to ask whether philosophers should be primarily, or even exclusively, descriptive metaphysicians, or not. But Strawson's own account of the distinction itself is by no means so straightforward. He goes on: '. . . there is a massive central core of human thinking which has no history—or none recorded in histories of thought; there are categories and concepts which, in their most fundamental character, change not at all. . . . It is with these, their interconnexions, and the structure that they form, that a descriptive metaphysics will be primarily concerned.'[5] That is, according to this more elaborate account of the distinction, certain concepts appear to be necessary (in some sense of 'necessary') to *every* set of concepts. It is the task of the descriptive metaphysician not merely to describe our conceptual scheme at any given time, but to pick out that part of it which is common to *every* scheme, that 'massive central core of human thinking'. The scope of revisionary metaphysics is therefore limited; certain concepts and categories, forming the core of any scheme, simply cannot change.

The revisionary metaphysician will surely complain (rightly) that to accept the elaborated distinction is to beg the question against him. It may be true that certain concepts must be part of *any* conceptual scheme but arguments must be offered to show that that is so. For example one might produce arguments of a Kantian kind to show that the concepts of an enduring material object and of a self-conscious person are mutually dependent and necessary features of any conceptual scheme of which we can coherently conceive. Strawson produces no argument of this kind; indeed he may even be open to the charge that the arguments he subsequently produces, in Chapters 1–3 of *Individuals*, demonstrate at most that the concepts of a person and a material object are fundamental to *our* conceptual scheme, but not necessarily to *any* scheme. It seems both unfair and unnecessarily restrictive at this stage of the inquiry to suppose that the revisionary metaphysician is engaged merely in remapping certain peripheral sections of our conceptual scheme. It is better to leave open the question whether he may successfully revise certain of our most fundamental concepts. Let us therefore adopt the original, unqualified distinction between descriptive and revisionary metaphysics and let us invite the revisionary metaphysician to propose, and justify, radical changes in our conceptual scheme.

It is interesting to note *en passant*—we shall return to the point again, in Chapters 7 and 8—that the distinction between two kinds of metaphysics brings with it a distinction between two kinds of analysis. The descriptivist is concerned to describe the general features of our concepts as we actually employ them, and we may expect him therefore to offer analyses which are logically equivalent to, or at any rate closely connected logically with, their analysanda. The revisionary metaphysician, on the other hand, may

[5] *Op. cit.*, p. 10.

be expected to offer analyses which are at best extensionally equivalent to their analysanda. For he is not concerned to give an account of the concepts which we employ, but rather to suggest concepts which do the same work rather better. Purists may refuse to regard revisionary 'analyses' as analyses at all, and may insist that extensional equivalence is at best a necessary, but by no means the only, relation between analysis and analysandum.

Purism may have its rewards but philosophical insight is not necessarily one of them. As long as we distinguish the method of revisionary metaphysics from that of descriptive metaphysics, it matters very little how we label them. To insist for example that an account of combustion could in no way yield an *analysis* of the concept of phlogiston is to miss the point of the proposal that one set of scientific concepts should replace another—and the proposal retains its philosophical interest, however we distribute our labels. Indeed, since the distribution of labels is not in itself important, I shall be quite happy to allow the revisionary metaphysician to describe his investigations as analytical.

Though the properties of the labels are not of interest, the properties of what is labelled most definitely are. And it is particularly important to notice that the scope and type of revision may vary from case to case. In certain cases it may seem appropriate to dispense with a concept entirely, as scientists once dispensed with the concept of phlogiston, or as Berkeley attempted to dispense with the concept of material substance. A second type of case is where it is appropriate in the interests of consistency merely to alter slightly the criteria of application of a certain concept— as happened for example when black 'swans' were first discovered. If the scope of the revision is very limited, we shall be inclined to say that we have retained the same concept but have revised certain of its criteria of application. A concept is too open-textured, so we tighten it up a little; or we find it too rigid and have to make it a little more flexible. A third closely related type of case is where it becomes appropriate to replace a concept by a different concept, for the scope of the revision is too spectacular to allow our talking only of changing the criteria of application of the original concept. Certain cases of so-called 'reduction' of one concept or another are cases of this kind—replacement of material object concepts by sense-datum concepts, replacement of the concepts of chemistry by those of physics, and so on. And finally, of course, it may be necessary to introduce a new concept, not to replace an old, useless concept but rather to enable us to talk about certain individuals which cannot otherwise be distinguished in any simple or precise way—for example we introduce the concept of a particle, or the Freudian concepts of the id, the libido, etc., or the economic concept of the multiplier, and so on.

Whatever the kind of revision envisaged, it is incumbent on the revisionary metaphysician to *justify* his proposals, to show that his revised conceptual framework is a better framework than the descriptive framework it is designed to replace. For example, he may claim that it is a more (internally) consistent framework, or that it coheres more exactly with certain scientific assumptions, or that it enables us to describe the world more precisely and comprehensively, and so on. An important consideration in deciding whether to accept the recommendations of the revisionary metaphysician will be the relative efficiency of the revised framework in helping to solve or dissolve philosophical perplexities. It is not sufficient of course that the revisionary metaphysician finds himself with *fewer* philosophical problems than does the descriptive metaphysician, since his freedom from philosophical puzzlement may have been obtained simply by his overlooking certain problems.

2. *The Problem*

So to the general problem with which I intend to wrestle in this book. We do not encounter only shoes, ships, sealing-wax, cabbages, and kings on our way around the world: more interestingly, we encounter people. And although we may wish to ask why the sea is boiling hot and whether pigs have wings, a philosophically more important problem may impress itself upon us—the problem of analysing the concept of a person. Not only is the concept of a person one of the most important, it is also one of the most plausible candidates for membership of that special group of concepts which according to Strawson is the 'massive central core of human thinking'. I propose, first, to offer a descriptive account of our concept of a person, a general account of the concept as we actually employ it. I then propose to set out perhaps the most significant revisionary account of people in what I take to be its most coherent form, namely the account based on the Identity Theory, the claim that mental states are identical with certain physical states. Having offered the two accounts I propose to attempt an answer to two questions: first, are the 'descriptive' and 'revisionary' accounts competitors?; and, second, if they are competitors, which account should we accept, and why?

It is unnecessary to rehearse in any detail the enormous budget of mind–body problems which these two questions introduce. They are familiar to every student of the subject. I shall only make one remark which will, I hope, clarify the problems a little and put the whole of what follows into perspective. Philosophers have been quick to observe that the expression 'mind–body' is decidedly unfortunate, for it suggests quite wrongly that something called a 'mind' is attached to something called a 'body', and that philosophers are concerned to show how precisely it is attached. That is, it suggests quite wrongly that Descartes was right in principle, if wrong in certain details. In fact the problem of the relation between mind and body, of analysing the concept of a person, arises from one very simple and non-tendentious observation, namely that human beings appear to have many properties which the rest of nature (with the exception of some animals) do not. They can think, act, perceive, feel certain emotions, and so on; trees, stones, tables cannot. To analyse the concept of a person is essentially to analyse these peculiar properties. Whether we call them 'mental' properties (or more disastrously, lumping them together, 'a mind') or not matters very little.

The two accounts of persons to be examined in this book offer quite different analyses. The first, the 'descriptive' account, insists that the peculiar properties of human beings are *logically* peculiar, that they cannot be reduced to properties shared by trees, stones, and tables, that the crucial component of the concept of a person (yielding the most important criterion of personal identity) is just that set of peculiar, 'mental', properties. The second, the 'revisionary' account, insists, however, that the apparent difference between human beings and inanimate things is only apparent, that these so-called peculiar properties can for the most part be reduced to the ordinary physical properties shared by trees, stones, and tables, that the main difference between humans and inanimate things is at best a difference of complexity. The second insists that humans are essentially continuous with the rest of nature, the first that (for philosophical purposes at any rate) they are not.

PART II

THE DESCRIPTIVE ACCOUNT

> Let observation with extensive view
> Survey mankind from China to Peru.
>
> (JOHNSON, *Vanity of Human Wishes*.)

2

PERSONS

1. *Method*

BEFORE embarking on the task I attributed to the descriptive
metaphysician, 'to describe the general features of, and relations
between, the concepts we employ in describing various individuals
in the universe of discourse', it is important to pick out the analytical tools available to him. It would be philosophically dishonest
to disguise their limitations. Unlike the revisionary metaphysician,
he cannot appeal to the facts of science except in so far as they are
reflected in our language; he cannot resolve inconsistencies in his
conclusions except in so far as they are due to errors in his reasoning. His whole argument consists fundamentally in an extended
appeal to our linguistic or logical intuitions, and those who find
such appeals unattractive may well contemplate the enterprise
with gloom. For appeals to our logical intuitions are often merely
invitations to wallow in traditional ignorance and confusion; our
language may in part reflect poor reasoning and superstition.
However, it is important to stress that at the moment we are concerned simply with *exposition* of the descriptive account, just as in
Part III we shall be concerned simply with *exposition* of the revisionary alternative. It is only in Part IV that we shall be contemplating the defence of each against the other.

2. *Persons*

As I observed, the labels 'descriptive' and 'revisionary' are
Strawson's, and his is the most important recent attempt to offer a
descriptive account of the concept of a person, in the third chapter
of *Individuals*. However, save for a few introductory remarks, I
do not intend to consider his account in any detail, for its principal
defects have already been pointed out most eloquently by, for
example, Ayer[1] and Cornman.[2] It is of course convenient to
adopt certain of his technical terms. In particular I shall talk of

[1] A. J. Ayer, 'Concept of a Person'.
[2] J. W. Cornman, 'Strawson's "Person" '.

'M-predicates' (those predicates ascribable both to persons and to material objects, like 'is heavy', 'is tall', 'is soft', etc.) and of 'P-predicates' (those ascribable only to persons and in certain cases animals, like 'is thinking', 'is in pain', 'is watching a football match', etc.). So it is P-properties which are what I call the peculiar properties of human beings, those properties which appear to distinguish them from inanimate things. As I implied at the end of the first chapter, it is rather better to talk about properties shared by all material things and properties peculiar to human beings than to talk about 'physical' and 'mental' properties; and likewise the distinction between M- and P-properties is not equivalent to a distinction between physical and mental properties. Consider for example a predicate like 'is drawing a picture' or 'is changing gear'. Drawing and driving certainly involve a great deal of physical movement but they are clearly properties peculiar to human beings. However, in the interests of brevity I shall occasionally distinguish 'physical' from 'mental' properties, and point out any difficulties which arise from conflating that distinction with the distinction between M- and P-properties.

It is also important to note that the distinction between M- and P-predicates or M- and P-properties is not as clear as one would wish.[3] At best one might say that the M-properties of a thing are essentially a function of its being spatio-temporal and P-properties a function of its being conscious. But that best is not very good, even if we take 'conscious' to mean 'capable of being conscious'. There are various predicates which do not fit very well into either group—most notably biological predicates like 'is growing', 'is mature', even 'is an adult'. We might say, I suppose, that 'is mature' is ambiguous, that it is an M-predicate when ascribed to a tree, a P-predicate when applied to a human being; we might, less plausibly, say that it is always an M-predicate. But do we not say that people are *emotionally* mature? It is fortunate that this is a difficulty which we can evade, simply by concentrating on predicates which clearly do fit into one group or another. 'Is solid', 'is made of green cheese', 'is wet', 'weighs sixteen stone', are clearly M-predicates; 'is thinking about philosophy', 'is in pain', 'intends to go to the pictures' are clearly P-predicates.

And so to Strawson. He wishes to argue that the concept of a

---

[3] I am indebted to Professor Ryle for this point and for some of the examples which follow.

person is logically primitive, and not that of an embodied mind, or animated body; there are not two kinds of thing, minds and bodies, but rather one logically irreducible kind of thing, persons, to whom are ascribed two kinds of property. The nearest one comes to talking of minds and bodies is in conceding that there are two kinds of property (M- and P-properties) and that some (namely the P-properties) may have two kinds of criteria of application. Now it is very striking that Strawson does not present us with a conclusive argument to prove that the concept of a person is logically primitive. Indeed at one point he almost gives the impression that such a claim is primarily a panacea for all our philosophical ills in this area: 'What we have to acknowledge, in order to begin to free ourselves from these difficulties, is the primitiveness of the concept of a person.'[4] Certainly if the concept of a person *is* primitive we *are* relieved of all the difficulties of Cartesianism, behaviourism, materialism, *et al.* But presumably there is rather more to be said than that.

However, there is an argument, admirably brief, on page 100 which might say rather more. It is designed to prevent the problem of other minds from arising and seems to be intended to show that the concept of a person is logically primitive: 'One can ascribe states of consciousness to oneself only if one can ascribe them to others. One can ascribe them to others only if one can identify other subjects of experience. And one cannot identify others if one can identify them *only* as subjects of experience, possessors of states of consciousness.' Essentially, that is, the concept of a person is primitive because P-properties are rather complex properties. For example a man may know he is miserable on the basis of certain 'inner' criteria (although, as Strawson remarks, it is very odd to talk of using *criteria* in one's own case), whereas we may know he is miserable on the basis of certain 'outer' criteria—his miserable expression, lethargic movements, inability to concentrate on anything for very long, and so on. There is one state of misery but two sets of criteria of application. If we are too obsessed (as Descartes was) with the 'inner' criteria we shall be tempted to treat persons essentially as minds; if we are too obsessed with the 'outer' we shall lapse into some physicalist alternative (e.g. radical behaviourism). If we remember there are *two* sets of criteria, but only *one* property, we can steer carefully between the two extremes.

[4] *Individuals*, p. 101.

We shall see that it is absurd to think of people as essentially physical or essentially mental or essentially a combination of both. P-properties are irreducible. They are neither 'mental' nor 'physical', although there are both 'mental' and 'physical' criteria of application. Since P-properties are irreducible, the concept of a person (that which has those properties) is logically primitive.

It has been pointed out by Ayer and Cornman that if we take the argument as simply an attempt to prevent the sceptic from raising the problem of other minds it fails, because it is invalid. But, more importantly for our purposes, even if it were valid, even if Strawson *had* shown that the problem of other minds cannot arise, it is by no means clear that he has thereby shown that the concept of a person is primitive. A Cartesian for example might argue that a person is so intimately united with his body that all our P-predicates span both the occurrence of certain states of consciousness *and* the occurrence of certain physical states. If the problem of other minds cannot arise, he will say, it is precisely because a man *is* so united with his body, sufficiently united to allow the use of predicates (viz. P–predicates) which have two quite different kinds of criteria of application. Certainly, he will concede, one cannot identify others if one can identify them only as subjects of experience: it is decidedly fortunate, albeit fortuitous, that we can identify them by identifying the bodies to which they are attached.

So I propose to present an argument to show rather more conclusively that the concept of a person is primitive, in the sense that it cannot be reduced to the concept of a mind or to that of a body or to any combination thereof. I shall present it in the form of five theses, or sets of theses, the first of which I shall approach by rehearsing the traditional objections to Cartesianism. The reasons for concentrating on Cartesianism are not merely that it is the most tempting solution of mind–body problems, but, more importantly, that the traditional objections to it use the resources of descriptive metaphysics. That is, they involve a series of appeals to our linguistic or logical intuitions—most notably to what we regard as category-sense and what we regard as category-nonsense. The difficulties in Cartesianism provide the best illustrations of the claims made in the first thesis.

One objection to Cartesianism is interesting but unhelpful. It is interesting to reflect that the Cartesian offers no guarantee that one body has only one mind, or indeed that one mind has but one body. It is unhelpful, for the Cartesian may claim that, although we have no logical guarantee that minds and bodies stand in a one–one relationship, we can fall back on an inductive guarantee, in so far as we have no reason to suppose they ever in fact stand in any other relationship. Our argument becomes more to the purpose if we reflect on a second objection. According to Descartes, 'to speak accurately I am not more than a thing which thinks, that is to say a mind or soul . . .'[5] It is a consequence of this position that there is an ambiguity in e.g. 'my' (and *mutatis mutandis* 'your', 'his', 'her', 'our', etc.) between its meaning in 'my mind' and its meaning in 'my body'—the difference between 'the mind *which is myself*' and 'the body *to which I am closely united*'. Similarly there are ambiguities of reference of personal pronouns, depending on whether they are coupled with P-predicates or with M-predicates. That there are ambiguities, as such, is not puzzling, for it is one of the obvious and fundamental features of referring terms and personal possessive adjectives that their reference may change from context to context, even from clause to clause, and that careless use of them provokes misunderstanding. We do not find it in the least puzzling that two different people both use 'I' to refer to themselves, 'my' and 'mine' to pick out their respective belongings, and so on. It is a particular sort of supposed ambiguity, in a particular context, that is puzzling. Suppose I say of Smith, 'He is standing by the apple-tree and is thinking about a problem.' The Cartesian must interpret me as saying, 'The body to which Smith is closely united is standing by the apple-tree, and Smith is thinking about a problem.' He must claim that we shall only suppose that P- and M-predicates are both ascribable to persons if we are misled by the superficial grammar of statements about people and/or their bodies. Deeper analysis will reveal that M-predicates are strictly speaking ascribable only to the bodies to which persons are united. The analysis of certain sentences containing P-predicates will be inordinately complicated. Those are sentences which contain P-predicates referring (explicitly or implicitly) both to certain 'inner' states and to certain 'outer' states or events. For example consider a sentence like 'He carefully painted the kitchen wall': this will turn out to

[5] Descartes, *Meditation* II (Haldane and Ross, Vol. I, p. 152).

be something of the form 'He reflected deeply on the problems of painting the kitchen wall, as the body to which he was attached drew a paint-brush to and fro across it.' Or 'he grimaced with pain' will be analysed as 'he felt an acute sensation of pain, and the face of the body to which he was attached screwed up.'

As descriptivists we may be excused a feeling of acute discomfort. Indeed it would seem that no one felt the discomfort more acutely than Descartes himself, when he realized that the separation of person and body was by no means as neat as he originally suggested:

Nature also teaches me by these sensations of pain, hunger, thirst, etc., that I am not only lodged in my body as a pilot in a vessel, but that I am very closely united to it, and so to speak so intermingled with it that I seem to compose with it one whole. For if that were not the case, when my body is hurt, I, who am merely a thinking thing, should not feel pain, for I should perceive this wound by the understanding only, just as the sailor perceives by sight when something is damaged in his vessel; and when my body has need of drink or food, I should clearly understand the fact without being warned of it by confused feelings of hunger and thirst. For all these sensations of hunger, thirst, pain, etc. are in truth none other than certain confused modes of thought which are produced by the union and apparent intermingling of mind and body.[6]

His own solution of the problem was certainly direct, if a little unphilosophical. Repeated promptings from the Princess Elizabeth of Bohemia finally elicited this comforting advice: 'It is by relying exclusively on the activities and concerns of ordinary life, and by abstaining from metaphysical meditation . . . that we can learn to apprehend the union of soul and body.'[7] When in difficulties, forget about them.

The descriptivist will, however, try rather harder. He will urge the Cartesian to take the 'intermingling' of mind and body more seriously, so seriously as in effect to abandon Cartesianism entirely. He will claim that, as our language is employed, it is entirely implausible to suggest that the systematic ambiguity thrust upon us by the Cartesian ever arises; it is implausible to suggest that the reference of e.g. 'I' in a particular context is ambiguous between

---

[6] Descartes, *Meditation* VI (Haldane and Ross, Vol. I, p. 192).

[7] Descartes, Letter to Princess Elizabeth of Bohemia, 28 June 1643 (*Descartes' Philosophical Writings*, ed. and trans. Kemp-Smith, pp. 274–5).

a person and a body, and that the ambiguity can be resolved only by deciding whether the predicate coupled with 'I' is a P- or an M-predicate. Turned round and expressed more strongly, this claim becomes the first main thesis of the descriptive account, namely that the reference in a particular context of a particular personal pronoun (or the meaning of a personal possessive adjective) is the same, whether coupled with an M- or a P-predicate. Thus, in 'He is standing by the apple-tree and he is thinking' the reference of 'he' in each case is in no way a function of the predicate coupled with it; assuming that it is quite clear that e.g. the two occurrences of 'he' do not refer to James and John respectively, their reference is clearly the same.

To approach the second and third main theses of the descriptive account we must introduce the notion of a category mistake. That is, we must assume that some expressions can be significantly coupled with others, and some not. For example, to state the second thesis straight off, both M- and P-predicates can be significantly, truly or falsely, coupled with terms referring to people. I can clearly say, truly or falsely, that John is lying down or that James is depressed, whereas I could not say that Jill is $\sqrt{(2)}$ or that Joan is a strong Verb, and so on. So far, perhaps, so good. But an interesting complication arises when we consider whether M- and P-expressions may be coupled together. The third thesis is that they cannot. That is, as our language works at the moment, the P-expression 'pain' cannot be coupled with the M-expression 'green'—'this pain is green' or 'green is in pain' are both nonsense. Similarly one cannot say 'This body is thinking about a cricket match' or 'His anger was six feet wide'. At the very best statements such as these are metaphorical and the force of the metaphor lies precisely in the deliberate flaunting of category-differences. At their worst they are nonsense. That is, in the 'formal' mode we might say that M-expressions and P-expressions cannot in general be significantly coupled together; or in the 'material' mode we might say that minds and bodies are different kinds of thing. On the whole, since category-differences do tend to cut right across one another and since it is therefore a little peculiar to talk of kinds of thing, I think that the 'formal' mode is better, that it is better to think of category-differences in terms of differences between kinds of expression, rather than between kinds of thing.

Before moving on we should consider two possible sources of complaint. First, it might be objected that the descriptivist is relying on a very woolly notion indeed in expressing his argument in the language of category-mistakes, that this dependence on the emperor's new clothes really will not do. In reply one can only repeat what was said at the start of the chapter. It is certainly true that no satisfactory criteria have ever been established for locating category-mistakes in a systematic fashion. But, on the other hand, in a purely *descriptive* account there is nothing particularly pernicious in our pointing out that, as our language actually works, members of one class of expressions cannot significantly be coupled with members of another class. Our aim at present is merely to describe our actual employment of a certain concept or concepts, however unsystematic such employment may be. The notion of a category may be somewhat imprecise and investigations with its analytical assistance may be a trifle clumsy. But the descriptivist realizes that the sort of conceptual scheme he must extract from language may be more than a trifle imprecise, clumsy, and even inconsistent.

The second complaint is concerned with the results rather than the method of the investigation. The descriptivist has claimed (in the second thesis) that both M- and P-predicates are ascribable to persons and (in the third) that M- and P-expressions are of different categories. It would seem that these two claims are mutually inconsistent; it would seem peculiar that we can couple 'James' with an M-expression and with a P-expression, but that the M- and P-expressions in question cannot be significantly coupled together. There are certainly cases of prima facie intransitivity— for example one can say 'The question is hard' and 'The bed is hard' but not 'The bed is a question'. But the difficulty is usually resolved by pointing to an ambiguity in one or other of the expressions employed—in this case an ambiguity in 'hard'.

I have not space to go into all the details of category-absurdity. But Sommers has already shown[8] that this sort of complaint is founded on the tempting but false assumption that one of the formation-rules of the language must be a transitivity-rule, that if one expression can be significantly coupled with a second, and the second with a third, the first can be significantly coupled with the third. The proof is fairly straightforward, if we consider a

[8] F. Sommers, 'Types and Ontology', pp. 344 ff.

'connected' language, that is, a language in which every term can *either* be significantly coupled with every other *or* with some term that can be significantly coupled with every other *or* with some term that can be significantly coupled with some term that can be significantly coupled with every other *or* . . . etc. The adoption for such a language (that is, for every natural language) of a transitivity rule simply entails that there are no category-mistakes at all, for every term can be significantly coupled with every other. The very notion of a category, of the significant coupling of terms, would collapse entirely because there would be no expression in the language which could not significantly be coupled with every other. The examples I have already used, and many others, show clearly that our own language is not of that kind, and that it is not governed by a transitivity rule. In short, the second and third theses of the descriptive account are mutually consistent.

We are now in a position to deduce a crucial fourth thesis from the conjunction of the first three. In order of presentation they were as follows:

1. The reference in a particular context of a personal pronoun (or the meaning of a personal possessive adjective) is the same, whether coupled with an M- or a P-predicate;

2. Both M- and P-predicates can be significantly (truly or falsely) coupled with terms referring to people;

3. M- and P-expressions (and *a fortiori* M- and P-predicates) are of different categories.

From these three theses taken together, the conclusion in which we are mainly interested can now be drawn:

4. The concept of a person is logically primitive, prior both to that of a mind, and to that of a human body.

It is important to note precisely what is meant by 'primitive' here. By saying that the concept of a person is logically primitive we are to be taken as saying only that it cannot be analysed in terms of that of a mind or of that of a body or of both. A person is not a mind-substance or a body-substance or a peculiar hybrid thereof. As we shall see in the following chapter, Strawson is inclined to mean rather more by 'logically primitive' than this, and we must beware of confusing his broader sense of the term with the rather narrower sense employed here.

It might be appropriate to end this section by sketching in the exact logical connection between 1, 2, and 3, on the one hand, and

4, on the other. Suppose for example that the concept of a person could be reduced in the Cartesian fashion to that of a mind. It would follow *either* that one could not couple personal pronouns with M-predicates (that his, 2 would be false) *or* that M- and P-predicates would be of the same category (that is, 3 would be false) *or* that the reference of personal pronouns varied, depending on whether they were coupled with M- or with P-predicates (that is, 1 would be false) *or* of course, all three. Parallel consequences follow from supposing that the concept of a person can be analysed in terms of that of a body. And the third possibility, that it can be analysed in terms of that of a mind and that of a body, together, is inconsistent *either* with thesis 1 *or* with thesis 3 *or* with both.

3. *Classification, Reidentification, and Personal Identity*

It is convenient and helpful to break off the argument at this point to review the general strategy of the descriptivist enterprise. When a philosopher claims to have analysed the concept of an X (whatever X might be) we expect him thereby to have stated the criteria of identity of Xs. But to talk of criteria of identity conceals an important ambiguity in 'identity' and its cognates, 'identify' and 'identification'. For when I claim to have identified an X, *either* I may be claiming to have discovered that it was an X, not a Y or a Z, *or* I may be claiming that it is the same X that I picked out yesterday. The policeman may want to know both whether the object I saw late at night was a burglar, not a cat or a telegraph-pole, and that it is identical with the third man from the left in today's identity parade. The philosopher must therefore provide answers to two kinds of question: What kind of thing is an X? And how do we determine whether *this* X is the same as *that*? To introduce a pair of very convenient labels, he must distinguish statements which *classify* ('Here is a burglar, not a cat or a tele-graph-pole') from statements which *reidentify* ('This man is identical with the burglar I saw last night').

It would of course be a peculiar world in which things could be classified but not reidentified, and one needs to qualify the distinction in a number of ways. First, classification seems to presuppose reidentification, for reasons offered by Kant in the *Critique of Pure Reason*: to use concepts of things at all, one must think of at least some things as persisting, as reidentifiable at a later time. Second, reidentification seems to presuppose classification, for the obvious reason that one can't classify for a second time without first classifying for a first. And, third, and perhaps most importantly, in classifying the sort of things which may be reidentified one is necessarily *counting* them, using concepts which have criteria of distinctness built into them. For example in classifying a thing as a cabbage I am not merely distinguishing one part of the world from the rest of the world, I am also counting the number of cabbages in this bit of the world. In contrast, in classifying a thing as red I am not counting anything, for the concept of red does not on its own yield any principle of counting. The point of these remarks is that one should not suppose that the problem of counting arises only when one is asking questions about reidentification. Clearly if the question of reidentifying Xs is to arise at all, then the concept of X must yield a principle of counting (as 'cabbage' does and 'red' does not); but if the question of reidentification has arisen, then the problem of counting has already arisen with the question of classification.

Many of the problems, therefore, we encounter in trying to reidentify something may already have turned up in trying to classify it, and this will be particularly true where the 'something' is a person. We must be very careful not to press the distinction between classifying and reidentifying too hard. Taking the qualifications into account, we must regard it at most as a distinction between two irretrievably connected questions—but two questions none the less. Applying the distinction in its qualified form to the matter in hand, it becomes clear that the first four theses of the descriptive account primarily constitute an answer to a request for a *classification*—What kind of thing is a person? But we are still without a specific answer to a possible request for criteria of *reidentification*—How precisely do we determine whether *this* person is the same person as *that*? The answer to a question of the first kind (How do I decide that this object is a person, not a cabbage or a table or Beethoven's last String Quartet?) will be that the object is a person if it possesses certain physical characteristics, exhibits signs of certain mental ability, and so on. And it might be suggested that the object's possessing a body of a certain kind will be of considerable importance in answering questions of the *first* kind, but that they will play only a small part in answering questions of the *second* kind. While an object's being a certain shape is standardly sufficient for its being a person, it does not follow that continuity of that body is standardly sufficient for the continuity of that person. As we shall see, the fifth thesis of the descriptive account attempts to present the suggestion more concisely.

But before stating the thesis we must examine in some detail the considerations which support it. The whole controversy over criteria of personal identity, of course, has generated far more heat than one would expect from my somewhat sly references to 'criteria of a physical kind', 'certain mental ability', and so forth, in the previous paragraph. But the disagreement is quite clear and fundamental, between those who wish to give special prominence to non-physical criteria of personal identity (to what I shall henceforth refer to as 'mental identity') and those who wish to give special prominence to physical criteria (to 'bodily identity').

The first of these positions has always been very popular. In one form it tempted Plato and Descartes, in another, Locke; it has received literary recognition (in Anstey's *Vice Versa*); and several attempts have been made to restate it coherently in modern philosophical journals.[9] The general reflection underlying the variations on this Cartesian theme is that in human relationships the way people think, feel, act, towards others is of greater importance than their bodily characteristics. The distinguishing feature of human beings in general is their *consciousness*, and the distinguishing feature of each individual human being is his individual consciousness (or, in less overtly Cartesian language, his particular series of states of consciousness). Although a man may suffer a spectacular change in his physical characteristics, we have no hesitation in continuing to regard him as the same person; a spectacular change in his mental characteristics, on the other hand, may incline us strongly to regard him as quite another person, as the tale of Dr. Jekyll and Mr. Hyde demonstrates. Of course we take advantage of the contingent fact of bodily continuity to identify our acquaintances. It would be tiresome to insist that one's friends should rehearse their life-histories whenever one meets them, to ensure that one is not misled by mere bodily continuity. But in most moral, social, and legal relationships, it is attitudes, feelings, thoughts, memories, which are of crucial significance: there is a very intimate link between mental identity (defined very loosely for the moment as a certain kind of continuity in a series of states of consciousness) and personal identity.

[9] Cf. J. Shaffer, 'Persons and their Bodies', and A. M. Quinton, 'The Soul'.

This becomes clear (the argument continues) if we reflect on a number of puzzle cases—Locke's prince and cobbler,[10] Shoemaker's Brown and Brownson,[11] Quinton's dismal Scot and cheerful Pole,[12] or Anstey's Mr. and Master Bultitude in *Vice Versa*. All these cases are essentially as follows: let us suppose that in February we meet two people, X and Y, whose bodies are B_x and B_y respectively. And suppose that when we next meet them, in March, the person identified as the owner of B_x exhibits all the character-traits, memories, etc. attributed to Y in February, and vice versa. The March owner of the body of the February Mr. Bultitude exhibits all the character-traits, memories, etc. of the February Master Bultitude, and vice versa. We have two ways of describing what has happened: first we might suppose that at about the end of February X and Y (Mr. and Master Bultitude) underwent radical changes in character, and that it is entirely accidental that the February X and March Y, in the one case, and the February Y and March X, in the other, exhibit identical character-traits. This explanation involves preserving at all costs a close link between bodily and personal identity. Or second, more plausibly, we might suppose that X and Y have simply exchanged bodies—the explanation elaborated entertainingly by Anstey. It is plausible because in the majority of human transactions (but clearly not all) we should treat the March owner of B_x in exactly the same way as we treated the February Y, and vice versa. In particular we should find that the March owner of B_x could recall all those things which the February Y was normally expected to recall, and vice versa. Master Bultitude's friends would no doubt prefer the company in March of the schoolboy with the adult body to that of the adult with the schoolboy's body, even though at first they might be a little unsettled by the change in his condition.

But, it might be objected, things are not so simple; the Bultitude case, if coherent at all, is a special case requiring special treatment. There are other, simpler, cases which incline us to a quite different solution of our difficulties, a solution which stresses the unbreakable link between bodily identity and personal identity. I have

[10] Locke, *Essay*, Bk. II, Ch. 27, Sect. 15. The case is expanded interestingly in Penelhum's *Survival and Disembodied Existence*, pp. 79 ff.

[11] S. Shoemaker, *Self-Knowledge and Self-Identity*, Ch. 1.

[12] A. M. Quinton, op. cit.

MBP—B

already pointed out how difficult Descartes found the separation of body from mind, for he discovered sensations (pain, hunger, and thirst) which could not simply be written off as states of a mind-substance, but seemed to possess an irreducibly physical element in them. The attempt to separate bodily identity from personal identity is equally futile, and the futility is a *logical* futility. For a man's facial expression, gestures, physical strength, tone of voice, general bearing, are as much a part of his identity as his thoughts, memories, feelings, attitudes, and so on. But they are undeniably characteristic of a particular *physical* body. Likewise it is simply false to suggest that in human relationships it is the way people think, feel, act towards one another, which is significant, and not their physical characteristics. Quinton[13] points out that there are relationships of an exclusively bodily kind which would survive a change of 'soul' but not a change of body—e.g. 'relations of a rather unmitigatedly sexual type', as he so charmingly puts it. And his own attempted solution of this difficulty (his suggestion that where concern with the 'soul' is wholly absent, there is no interest in individual identity at all, only in identity of type) is at best an evasion.

If we are to believe Puccetti[14] this particular difficulty is not very serious. At most it shows that those who feature in exchanges of bodies may have to reconcile themselves to a new life without certain of their former physical abilities or oddities. In the most embarrassing sort of case a man may even have to get used to being female. (Puccetti is of course concerned with changes of brains rather than changes of minds, but the difficulty in question is common to both cases.) However, a more concise and coherent argument might be adduced to show that bodily identity is at the very least necessary for personal identity. Formally it is no better or worse than the Bultitude argument above, in that it consists in a straightforward appeal to our logical intuitions, to what we should or should not want to say in certain circumstances. In its most persuasive form it has been put forward by Williams,[15] who asks us to suppose that a man, Charles, undergoes a radical change of character, such that he claims to have witnessed and done a

[13] Op. cit., pp. 403–4.

[14] R. Puccetti, 'Brain Transplantation and Personal Identity'.

[15] B. A. O. Williams, 'Personal Identity and Individuation'; cf. also his 'Bodily Identity and Continuity: a Reply'. His position in 'The Self and the Future' seems to leave rather more room for a change-of-bodies case.

substantial number of the things Guy Fawkes apparently witnessed and did. Certainly, he argues, there is a strong temptation to say that Charles is Guy Fawkes. But on the other hand, he points out, if such radical changes can happen to Charles, they can also happen to his brother Robert, who can *also* claim to have witnessed and done all that Guy Fawkes witnessed and did. But if Charles is identical with Guy Fawkes, so, by parity of reasoning, is Robert. So Charles and Robert are identical, which is absurd. And the conclusion we are expected to draw from these considerations is that bodily identity is a necessary condition of personal identity; our reluctance to say that Charles and Guy Fawkes are the same person is due to our implicitly insisting that they must at least share the same body to count as the same person.

So we have the two main—mutually inconsistent—solutions to the problem of personal identity. The first suggests that mental identity is sufficient (but not necessary) for personal identity (it cannot be necessary, because a person's character may change radically as the result of a shock, he may fall into a coma, etc.); the second suggests that bodily identity is necessary for personal identity. It is important to see that the two solutions *are* mutually inconsistent. Let us therefore take the Bultitude case as a test case, describing it in neutral terms (i.e. in the way I described it earlier). If mental identity is sufficient for personal identity we must conclude that Mr. and Master Bultitude have simply exchanged bodies; if bodily identity is necessary for personal identity it cannot be the case that they have changed bodies with each other.

The fifth thesis of the descriptive account attempts to do justice to the virtues of both solutions, to state fairly explicitly our reasons for choosing to interpret the Bultitude case as a change-of-body case and yet to refuse to identify Charles and Guy Fawkes. Essentially it consists in accepting *both* that mental identity is sufficient for personal identity *and* that there is a presumption that bodily identity is necessary and sufficient for personal identity. Inconsistency is avoided by insisting that in certain cases (e.g. the Bultitude case) the latter presumption may be defeated, because the conditions for mental identity are so strikingly fulfilled. More formally:

5. Mental identity is sufficient but not necessary for personal identity; bodily identity is both defeasibly sufficient and defeasibly necessary for personal identity.

In all normal cases, and in the Charles/Guy Fawkes case, there will be no question of defeating the presumption that bodily identity is necessary and sufficient for personal identity.

Perhaps two points need to be noted before we round off the chapter. First it is necessary to emphasize (as I observed earlier) that mental identity is not necessary for personal identity. There is nothing absurd in the thought of a man's character changing completely and radically or of his suffering complete amnesia or of his going senile or (e.g. after serious brain damage) of his mental life, his 'stream of thought', as James so graphically describes it,[16] coming to an end completely. There are many actual cases of this kind which give no jolt to our notion of personal identity.

Second, we must come a little more firmly to grips with the notions of defeasible sufficiency and defeasible necessity. Logicians will probably treat them with scepticism, although legal philosophers, with an eye on the difficulties of legal practice, have already adopted them in one form at least.[17] Quite simply, if we have two conditions, one sufficient, one defeasibly sufficient (and/or defeasibly necessary), and their joint fulfilment leads to contradiction, the conclusion supported by the defeasibly sufficient condition is withdrawn. In the case in hand, where the joint application of the criterion of mental identity and the criterion of bodily identity leads to contradiction, the criterion of bodily identity is to be discarded.

It might be thought suspicious that my introducing the notion of a defeasibly sufficient condition appears to ease some of the difficulties surrounding personal identity which I sketched earlier. For it seems we can reconcile the strong arguments in favour of the bodily identity criterion with the equally strong inclination to accept the Bultitude case as a change-of-bodies case. But it would be unfair, I think to be too sceptical of the reconciliation, for, as I have already pointed out, lawyers operate in practice with a notion of defeasible sufficiency (even though they may not call it so). The legal system being as it is, proof that a man has driven in a certain manner in a certain place is defeasibly sufficient for his being found guilty of dangerous driving and punished. It is only *defeasibly* sufficient because the presumption that he is guilty

[16] W. James, *Principles of Psychology*, Vol. I, Ch. 9.
[17] Cf. H. L. A. Hart, 'The Ascription of Responsibility and Rights', pp. 174–183.

and should be penalized may be defeated. If he is shown to have been suffering from a sudden illness (such as a heart-attack) which made him unable to control the car properly, he will not be found guilty of dangerous driving; if he is an ambulance driver, with an otherwise admirable record, who was attempting at the time to drive an injured man to hospital, he may be found guilty but discharged. One set of facts yields a presumption that he is guilty and should be penalized; others, the extenuating circumstances, defeat it in whole or in part. Similarly, in the Bultitude case, one set of facts (about bodily continuity) yields a certain presumption; others (about apparent mental continuity) may defeat it. Just as we find in one case that extenuating circumstances carry more weight than the prima facie facts of the case, so in the other we may find that the mental identity criterion may carry more weight than the bodily identity criterion.

It might be objected that I have merely demonstrated conclusively that the confusions surrounding my analysis of personal identity also afflict practising lawyers. It might be claimed that the notion of a defeasibly sufficient condition is as cloudy now as when I first introduced it. But there is, I think, an answer to this renewal of the sceptical attack on our logical apparatus, an answer which draws attention to the *clarity* of the notion of defeasible sufficiency, its *precision* as an analytical tool, compared with the notion it is intended to replace. For it is of course intended to do the work which is usually done by the notion of a *criterion*. Philosophers have talked about criteria of personal identity, criteria of goodness, criteria of freedom, and so on, but have been a little puzzled about the criteria of being a criterion. One thing only has always been clear: standardly, if a certain condition is a criterion of another, then the relation between the fulfilment of the first (antecedent) condition and the fulfilment of the second (consequent) is stronger than that of material (truth-functional) implication and weaker than that of entailment. That is, on the one hand, the connection between a man's performing acts of charity and his being a good man is stronger than the connection between my writing these words now and two plus two's being four; on the other hand, it is not straightforwardly self-contradictory (although it may be peculiarly absurd) both to assert that a man performs acts of charity and that he is not a good man.

We might note the qualification 'standardly', for in certain cases the criterial relation becomes virtually indistinguishable from the relation of entailment (e.g. the criterial relation between a knife's being sharp and its being a good knife). But on the whole the notion of a criterion occupies the logical limbo between that of material implication and that of entailment. And as long as the limbo is left in such a sorry state a number of difficulties remain unsolved. It is not clear for example how the joint assertion of the antecedent and denial of the consequent of a proposition claiming a certain criterial relation to hold is peculiarly absurd, though not self-contradictory; it is not clear how there can be a vast range of heterogeneous and often conflicting criteria of (e.g.) goodness or personal identity; it is not clear how and, more importantly, why conflicts between criteria are resolved in favour of one criterion rather than another. I cannot claim to have solved these problems by talking of defeasibly sufficient conditions rather than criteria. In particular it is no more clear where exactly in the logical limbo we must place our defeasibly sufficient conditions than where exactly we must place our criteria. But by making explicit the crucial notion of defeasibility we do make it clear how there can be a range of heterogeneous criteria/defeasibly sufficient conditions of (e.g.) goodness or personal identity, how and why conflicts between them are resolved. Just as in the law courts we allow extenuating conditions to defeat a prima facie presumption of guilt, so we allow certain conditions to override certain others in our resolution of problems of personal identity.

4. *A Sixth Thesis, and Provisional Conclusion*

There is still one lacuna in the formal statement of descriptivism which needs to be filled. We have been talking so far of various criteria of identity—mental, bodily, personal—in an attempt to distinguish and relate them. But so far we have not mentioned a further very important identity, the identity of states of consciousness, of experiences, although in a sense it has been lurking beneath the surface of the whole argument of the chapter. Thesis 6, then, will be as follows:

6. The connections between a particular person and a particular set of experiences, *qua* experiences of a certain type or types, is contingent; the connection between a particular person and a particular set of experiences, *qua* particular experiences, is necessary. The contrast between the first and the second parts of the thesis

can be brought out as follows. It is certainly contingent that my experiences are, say, of visual impressions of a garden or sensations of pain, for they might have been auditory impressions of an explosion or sensations of tickling. Indeed it is entirely contingent that they occur at all. But it is *necessary* that if they occur at all they occur as *mine*. It cannot be contingent that my states of consciousness are mine, as it is contingent that my car is mine. There is a perfectly obvious way in which my car (identified as the car of a certain colour, registration number, etc.) could have been someone else's, because someone else might have entered into an appropriate contract of sale before I did so. But there is no way in which a particular experience of mine could have been someone else's. Either this particular experience of mine is mine or it is not an experience at all, i.e. it is not. As Kant pointed out with such force, consciousness entails self-consciousness; the notion of a heap of unowned experiences is straightforwardly absurd: 'It must be possible for the "I think" to accompany all my representations; for otherwise something would be represented in me which could not be thought at all, and that is equivalent to saying that the representation would be impossible, or at least would be nothing to me.'[18] And if nothing to me then nothing at all.

So much then for thesis 6. But in reviewing the whole course of the descriptive enterprise so far we may still have considerable doubts about thesis 5, which consisted in the claim that bodily identity is defeasibly sufficient and defeasibly necessary for personal identity and that mental identity is sufficient but not necessary for personal identity. It was intended to give formal expression to apparently conflicting interpretations of two puzzle cases, the Bultitude case and the Charles/Guy Fawkes case. It seemed that the considerations which led us to describe the Bultitude case as a change-of-body case were flatly inconsistent with those which led us to deny the identity of Charles and Guy Fawkes. Now it is quite clear that thesis 5 allows us to describe the Bultitude case as a change-of-body case; it is by no means clear that it also allows us to deny the identity of Charles and Guy Fawkes. For if the presumption that bodily identity is necessary for personal identity can be defeated when it appears to conflict with the presumption that mental identity is sufficient, then it would seem we have to say that Charles is indeed identical with Guy Fawkes.

---

[18] Kant, *Critique of Pure Reason*, B. 131.

The only other immediate solution of the difficulty was open to us even before all the talk of defeasible conditions, namely that Charles is in no way *mentally* identical with Guy Fawkes.

However, before we can come to fresh grips with Charles and Guy Fawkes we must be quite clear that we know what 'bodily identity' and 'mental identity' mean. It may be that a solution of our difficulties will emerge from clarifying them. The first, 'bodily identity', presents no serious problems: when we talk of bodily identity we are talking simply of the spatio-temporal continuity of a certain physical object (namely, a human body). It is with the second that serious difficulties arise, difficulties which, as we have seen, threaten to undermine the whole fabric of the descriptive account. So we must enter the second stage of the argument, the attempt to clarify the notion of a temporally continuous mind. The declension from persons into minds will no doubt be comforting to the Cartesian, but he may be a trifle disappointed by its execution in the following chapter. As I have already pointed out, we should not think of body-mind problems as problems about the way one thing, a body, is attached to another, a mind. 'The mind' is only a convenient label for all those states, dispositions, activities, abilities ascribed by the use of P-predicates. Most particularly, as we shall see, it is a convenient label for a series of states of consciousness.

3

MINDS

1. *Introductory*

IT is with a certain amount of trepidation that we approach the next stage of the descriptive account, for the history of philosophy is strewn with vain attempts to analyse the notion of a temporally continuous mind. A fundamental difficulty which has vitiated many of them has been that the expression 'mental' and its cognates cover a much larger logical area than philosophers have acknowledged. There has been a very tempting tendency to suppose with the empiricists that the mind consists essentially of the immediate contents of consciousness, of 'impressions' or 'ideas' and copies or complexes of them. Wittgenstein and his disciples were quick to point out that many so-called 'mental' activities cannot be analysed in terms of the overt physical symptoms of covert states of consciousness, that they are intelligible only as operations subject to certain rules or conventions, within a certain context—operations which frequently do not even *require* the occurrence of characteristic states of consciousness.

We do not need to pursue some of the disciples into analytical behaviourism; there is no need to claim that there are no states of consciousness. The most we should and must claim is that some P-predicates refer entirely, some refer in part, to the occurrence of states of consciousness, and some refer to operations which do not involve characteristic states of consciousness at all. More generally we may be permitted a distinction between those mental activities in which the occurrence of states of consciousness is of paramount importance, and those in which it is not—with the qualification that the area in between will be very hazy. The activities of the second group will become of crucial importance later on but at the moment the descriptivist is interested only in those of the first. He has throughout his argument stressed that the crux of the mind–body problem is the occurrence of states of consciousness. For it to be intelligible to talk of mental activities at all (he will say), whether of the first or of the second group, it is necessary that persons be conscious; and in resolving disputes about personal identity the contents of consciousness are of considerable importance. So in attempting to provide a logical prop for his claims about the criteria of personal identity he begins with the materials with which Hume began his analysis of the mind. The other materials, the states and activities which do not refer (wholly or in part or at all) to the occurrence of characteristic states of consciousness, will turn up again in the course of the argument.

I must emphasize again, incidentally, that talking of 'minds' does not commit one to any kind of Cartesian, substantialist, position. Indeed since the descriptivist claims that the concept of a person is primitive, he must avoid Cartesianism at all costs. There are other, more general, reasons of course: even if we admitted that it is significant to talk of a mind-substance, the only criteria we should have for identifying a particular mind-substance would be precisely those criteria we have for identifying a particular series of states of consciousness. We could not for example identify a mind-substance which had no inhering states of consciousness. Just as Hume complained (tongue in cheek) that he could never discover his real self without bumping into a state of consciousness which thereby obscured it, so we should note that it is impossible to identify a mind-substance save in so far as we can identify a series of states of consciousness. That being so, it is entirely gratuitous to postulate a mind-substance at all. So in referring to a temporally continuous mind we shall for the moment be referring only to a certain connected series of states of consciousness, related to one another in certain ways still to be determined.

Perhaps we might also note *en passant* that the word 'mind' and its cognate 'mental' have already been used in three different ways; it is hardly surprising that discussions of mind–body problems are so muddy. First, I have talked and will continue to talk, very loosely, of mental states and activities, where 'mental' qualifies any state or activity ascribed by a P-predicate. Second, I have mentioned minds in the very narrow Cartesian sense of 'mind'—non-physical substances, things. And third, I am for much of this chapter going to use 'mind' in another rather narrow way, to refer only to series of states of consciousness—'minds' in the classical empiricist sense. The first and third senses will be used most frequently in this book, and they are quite clearly different. The first certainly includes, but is not included by, the third. A man who is fast asleep or who has forgotten an appointment is certainly in a mental state in the first sense (i.e. a certain P-property can be ascribed to him) but may not be in a mental state in the third sense (he may not be in a state of consciousness).

2. *Qualitative Continuity*

So then to minds in the third, Humean, sense, to the attempt to clarify the notion of a temporally continuous mind, a temporally continuous connected series of states of consciousness. In the previous chapter I referred to a distinction between problems of classification and problems of reidentification. Problems of classification are posed by questions of the form, is this a person (or a fish or a table or $\sqrt{(2)}$)? And problems of reidentification by questions of the form, is *this* person (at t_1, in February, on the racecourse) the same as *that* (at t_2, in March, who broke the bank at Monte Carlo)? To begin the investigation of mental identity we are to suppose that answers to a number of questions of the first kind—of classification—have been given. That is, suppose we have a normal human body B_x in front of us for rather a long period of time (t_0, t_1, t_2, t_3 . . . t_n). On ordinary physical criteria, we may suppose, we decide at t_0 that we have in front of us a person—let us call him X_0—whose body is B_x; he will presumably be having certain states of consciousness (if t_0 is not *too* short). Likewise we decide at t_1 that we have in front of us a person X_1, whose body is B_x, and who has certain states of consciousness; we decide at t_2 that we have a person X_2, whose body is B_x, and who . . .; and so on. We are quite clear we have a person at t_0 (not a cabbage or a page of Euclid), that we also have a person at t_1 (with similar qualifications), one at t_2 . . .; and so on. But (and this is the vital point) we leave open entirely the question whether X_0 is the *same* person as X_1, X_2, X_3 . . . X_n. That question can only be answered by trying to establish certain continuities between the states of X_0 at t_0 and those of X_1 at t_1, X_2 at t_2 . . . etc.

Matters may become very complicated indeed. Apart from our consuming interest in B_x we may also enjoy the company of other bodies, B_y and B_z . . . etc. We may identify Y_0 as the possessor of B_y at t_0; Y_1 at t_1, Y_2 at t_2 . . . etc. The general enterprise consists in trying to isolate each series of states of consciousness as constituting a single mind, and to argue that the identity of the mind in question is sufficient for the identity of the corresponding members of the series X_0, X_1, X_2, X_n . . . (or, in puzzle cases, perhaps X_0, Y_1, Z_2 . . . X_n . . . etc.).

However, it might be objected that it is pointless even to begin, because the enterprise is entirely circular. In the previous chapter it was pointed out that it is logically absurd to claim that my states of consciousness might have been yours; the criteria of identity of states of consciousness are logically tied to those of their owner. My states of consciousness are identified as mine, yours as yours, and so on. But if this claim is to be maintained (the objection continues) then the whole enterprise of this chapter is vacuous. We propose to identify certain persons by establishing certain continuities in a series of states of consciousness; but we can identify the states of consciousness only as the states of a certain person. The circularity is obvious and vicious: we can identify a person only by first identifying him.

The answer to the objection is straightforward, for it rests squarely on a confusion of two senses of 'identify'—on a confusion, that is, of problems of classification and problems of reidentification. Let us suppose that at t_0 X_0 has a certain experience or state of consciousness e_0 and that X_1 has e_1 at t_1, X_2 e_2 at t_2 . . ., and so on. Now the requirements of identity of states of consciousness certainly dictate that e_0 is necessarily X_0's, e_1 X_1's, e_2 X_2's, and so on. This is what we mean by 'identifying' X_0's experiences as *his*, X_1's as *his*, X_2's as *his*, and so on. But to say merely that e_0 is necessarily X_0's, e_1 X_1's, and so forth, does not presuppose an answer to the question, is X_0 the same as X_1, X_2, . . . etc.? For *that* question is a request for reidentification, the answer to which is given by answering the question, is e_0 continuous with (or a member of the same series as) e_1, e_2, e_3, . . .? The apparent circularity vanishes as soon as we realize that our 'identification' of e_0, e_1, e_2, . . . etc. requires the solution of a problem of *classification*, namely, is X_0 a person (or a cabbage or $\sqrt{(-1)}$)? It presupposes no solution at all of a problem of *reidentification*, namely, is X_0 the same person as X_1, X_2, X_3, . . . etc.?

We must now offer a possible solution, or series of solutions, to the problem of reidentification. But before doing so it is necessary to introduce a slight complication. In describing the materials for the inquiry so far, I have referred to the states of consciousness of X_0 at t_0, of X_1 at t_1, and so on. Clearly t_0, t_1, etc. must be regarded as 'specious presents', instants of time short enough to be picked out by the expression 'now' but long enough to cover the occurrence of most states of consciousness. We cannot and should not expect any more precise account of the specious present. In certain cases we might want to regard it as extending for only a split second, in others for several minutes. If then these are to be our materials, the items which are putatively to constitute a single continuous mind will not necessarily be states of consciousness, but will rather be *groups* of them. It is quite possible for example that at t_0 X_0 has a pain-sensation, a visual perception of a tree, and a thought about his dinner, and so on. The problem will be to relate this *group* of experiences to the *group* ascribed to X_1 at t_1, or Y_2 at t_2, or Z_3 at t_3. Grice once talked of a 'total temporary state' (t.t.s.): '. . . "experiences E and E' belong to the same t.t.s." means "E and E' would, given certain conditions, be known, by memory or introspection, to be simultaneous".'[1] From what I have said about the difference between problems of classification and problems of reidentification it is clear that we cannot embrace the suggestion as it stands, for any reference to memory presupposes a solution to a problem about reidentification. Questions of the form, what does X_0 introspect, on the other hand, pose no such problem. So we must say merely that E and E_1 belong to the same t.t.s. if and only if they would (given certain conditions) be known by introspection to be simultaneous. It remains only to propose that we talk of 'experience-clusters' rather than 'total temporary states' (for it is easier to remember what 'experience-cluster' means) and we may at last set off. Thus, if at t_0 X_0 is in pain and thinking about his dinner, his awareness of pain and his thought will be parts of the same experience-cluster. And we may then regard experience-clusters as the members of the series which putatively constitutes a single mind. Let us call such a series S and the experience-clusters which are its members e_0, e_1, e_2, . . . etc.

We are now at last able to attempt an analysis of mental identity. The first criterion of mental identity is perhaps the more obvious of the two we shall consider—although it is not perhaps quite so perspicuous as many of its proponents would seem to think. It is the criterion of qualitative continuity between the members of S (the series of experience-clusters which putatively constitutes a single mind). It is not quite so perspicuous as might be thought

[1] H. P. Grice, 'Personal Identity', p. 344.

because the notion of similarity on which it rests is more than a little vague. But the general point of talking about qualitative continuity is clear. One of the things which determines a man's identity is his character and personality, the way he thinks and feels about this, that, and the other, his interests, and so on. If there are certain similarities between a man's character and personality today and his character and personality last week, I have a way of showing that he is the same man as the man I met last week. His personality may change of course, but as long as the changes occur fairly gradually I have a way of reidentifying him from time to time. These are the sorts of considerations which inspired me to describe the Bultitude case as a change-of-bodies case: crudely, the interest in the Stock Exchange and the duties of paternity crossed from one body to the other, the enthusiasm for conkers and adventure stories crossed from the other to the one.

So we want to formalize our interest in certain continuities of character and personality, certain similarities between one experience-cluster and a second, between the second and a third, and so on. We are not of course interested in *all* such similarities, because some will be very trivial. We are not interested in experiences' being similar in that they are both experiences or in that they both last five seconds. Nor do we want to be blinded by the word 'continuity' and concentrate on the temporal succession of e_0, e_1, e_2, etc. to the exclusion of all else. To do any of these things is to generate an entirely fatuous series (my thoughts about qualitative continuity at t_0, the Prime Minister's anger at the Leader of the Opposition at t_1, the pain-sensation of an invalid in Hongkong at t_2, and so on). A very rough way of separating the trivial from the important would be to say that we are interested in similarities of *content* between experience-clusters. We are interested in their being similar in so far as they include thoughts about the First World War or feelings of anger at the state of the nation or expectations about the next conker season, and so on.

Having said that, let us try to formalize the criterion of qualitative continuity. The first step is to define a compound relation Q which holds between the experience-clusters which make up S. Thus, an experience-cluster e_0 stands in Q to another e_1 if and only if:

(a) e_0 and e_1 are similar in content, and

(b) e_0 precedes e_1.

Clearly Q is not transitive, for although the relation of temporal succession is transitive, that of similarity of content is not. For example e_0 may be similar to e_1 in that both include pain-experiences; e_1 and e_2 may be similar in that both include thoughts about Napoleon; but there is no necessary similarity between e_0 and e_2. As we shall see, this non-transitivity helps us (paradoxically) to bring out the full force of the expression 'continuity'.

The first criterion of mental identity, then, is as follows. The series S constitutes a single mind if it is possible to give a list of some of the members of S such that:

(i) the list is of pairs of members of S, the terms of each pair being related by Q—let us call these Q-pairs;

(ii) the Q-pairs are arranged so that the first term of the first Q-pair is the first member of S, and the second term of the last Q-pair is the last member of S; and

(iii) the Q-pairs are arranged so that the second term of each Q-pair is also the first term of the succeeding Q-pair (with the exception of the first term of the first Q-pair, and the second term of the last).

Translated into English, the criterion consists in a proposal that mental identity is preserved if a man's character-traits, dispositions, emotional responses, etc., change piecemeal, not all at once. (Of course, since it is designed to offer a solution to questions of personal identity via an analysis of mental identity, it does not refer either explicitly or implicitly to 'a man'.) Each member of at least a certain sub-set of S (a sub-set which includes both the first and last members of S) resembles the preceding member in some respect and the succeeding member in some respect; but this is not to demand that the member which precedes it resembles the member which succeeds it in any significant respect. This is the whole point of talking of qualitative *continuity* between the members of S.

Unfortunately the suggestion withers under close examination. It is immediately obvious that qualitative continuity is not a *necessary* condition of mental identity. For example a man might suffer a radical change in character and yet be able to remember everything he did before the change. We should want to say that mental identity through time had been preserved, even though there was a complete break in qualitative continuity.

Conversely it is not even clear that, as formulated, the criterion provides a *sufficient* condition of mental identity. The suggestion is that the series S constitutes a single mind if it is possible to give a list of *some* of the members of S such that the three stated conditions are fulfilled—that is, as long as a certain sub-set of the members of S exhibit the appropriate qualitative continuity. At least two difficulties spring to mind. The first is that the principle of membership of S has not been completely stated. It would seem that, as long as a certain qualitative continuity exists between certain experience-clusters, we can tack on as many other experience-clusters as we wish, and still label the whole series a single mind. Thus, if e_1, e_2, and e_3 are qualitatively continuous I am perfectly free to decide that the mind of which they are the most significant part is formed from e_1, e_2, e_3, e_4, e_5, *or* from e_0, e_1, e_2, e_3, e_n, *or* from any other combination in which e_1, e_2, and e_3 appear. Freedom of choice may be an advantage in certain contexts but is wholly inappropriate here.

The second difficulty also arises from our concentrating on only a *sub-set* of members of S. Suppose we have two series of experience-clusters, S and S'; that a sub-set of members of S are temporally coincident and qualitatively identical with a sub-set of members of S'; but that the other members of S have nothing in common with the other members of S'. It would seem peculiar to claim that S and S' are the same series and that they both constitute the same mind. But as the criterion of qualitative continuity now stands we have no way of distinguishing them. Since we are to concentrate solely on the qualitative identity of some members, but not all, of S and S', we are committed to the claim that the relevant sub-set of S is identical with the relevant sub-set of S', and that S and S' constitute the same mind.

We can of course evade the difficulties by strengthening the criterion. That is, instead of concerning ourselves with a sub-set of S, we must concern ourselves with all the members of S. The revised criterion will then be as follows. The series S constitutes a single mind, if it is possible to list *all* the members of S such that . . . (with conditions (i)–(iii) as before). We no longer have any freedom of choice as to which experience-clusters are to be included in which minds and we are no longer committed to the conflation of two clearly distinct series of states of consciousness.

The gains of our endeavour are unfortunately outweighed by two corresponding losses. The first difficulty is similar to the first of those we have just eradicated. But whereas we were previously (and absurdly) free to include any experience-cluster whatever in a certain temporally continuous mind, we are now (and equally absurdly) unable to include certain experience-clusters that we shall most certainly want to include. Suppose for example that in *S* there is an experience-cluster which bears no relevant similarities to any other (consisting in a unique twinge of toothache, a unique visual perception, a unique emotional response, etc.). Our revised criterion offers no instructions whatever for including it in *S*. Unless a man can contrive to repeat all his states of consciousness he will be unable to self-ascribe certain of them. Or, to put it another way, it may be plausible to claim that the revised criterion yields a sufficient condition of mental identity, but at the cost of triviality: we have to leave out certain very important factors.

The second difficulty is likewise similar to the second of the difficulties we have just evaded, namely a difficulty about the qualitative reduplication of series of experiences. There seems no contradiction in supposing that there might be two (or even more) qualitatively identical and temporally coincident series of experience-clusters (i.e. identical in number of members, temporal intervals between corresponding members, properties of corresponding members, and so on). Yet not merely does the revised criterion not provide us with a means of distinguishing one series from the other, it invites us to conflate them into one, to treat them as constituting one mind.

It might be suggested that this second difficulty stems from the inadequacy of our criteria of states of consciousness; that is (it might be said), we could and should stipulate that if it appears that there are two series, qualitatively identical and temporally coincident in the relevant way, we should treat them as *one*, as numerically identical. But I doubt whether this suggestion would do the trick. The problem of complete reduplication of experiences is perhaps a rather academic one (which we shall pursue later in the chapter) but the question of partial reduplication is not. One man's sensations and perceptions are very much like another's; we all feel very much the same kinds of toothache, see the same kinds of houses, trees, and so on. If qualitative continuity is to be sufficient for personal identity, then Smith and I shall be the same person if we both have toothache or if we both watch the same film from similar points of view.

There is no point in pursuing qualitative continuity any further. We have pointed to so many weaknesses that we are entitled to abandon it and try again elsewhere. It is quite clear that it yields neither a necessary nor a sufficient condition of personal identity. One may feel a certain reluctance to abandon completely a suggestion with which philosophers have toyed for so long, but it is unfortunately very clear that, however much they toy with it, they will not make it philosophically satisfactory.

3. Sensible Continuity

So we turn to fresh woods and pastures new, having made little progress in the analysis of mental identity. Perhaps on general grounds it is not surprising that an attempted analysis in terms of certain similarities between experiences came so spectacularly to grief, for we have a rather incoherent feeling that it is not the *qualitative* continuity of a series of experiences which makes it a single mind but rather a continuity of consciousness. It does not matter whether my pains, visual perceptions, thoughts, are similar to Smith's or different; what matters is whether or not we share the same consciousness. Nor does it matter very much whether my experiences now are qualitatively continuous with my experiences a month ago or a month hence; what matters is whether the same consciousness has been preserved throughout.

The second criterion of mental identity, the criterion of sensible continuity, is designed to give coherent expression to our feelings in this matter. Once again perhaps it is appropriate to issue a warning against interpreting 'consciousness' as a thing, a substance, as Descartes did. 'Consciousness' here is to be unpacked only as sensible continuity, as a set of complex relations between a series of experience-clusters. To get a general intuitive grasp of the notion of sensible continuity we might recall what William James had to say about it, for it is he who can most reasonably claim to have been the first to explore it in any detail:

The proposition that within each personal consciousness thought feels continuous, means two things:
1. That even where there is a time-gap the consciousness after it feels as if it belonged together with the consciousness before it, as another part of the same self;
2. That the changes from one moment to another in the quality of the consciousness are never absolutely abrupt.[2]

[2] W. James, *Principles of Psychology*, Vol. I, p. 237.

I said that the suggestion will help us to get a general intuitive grasp of the notion of sensible continuity, but it will not, I fear, do much more. Since James's interests were psychological rather than philosophical, since indeed he would have been reluctant to distinguish so clearly psychological from philosophical problems, the chapter from which the quotation is taken can best be regarded as a series of interesting suggestions, of provoking comments, rather than a connected philosophical analysis of sensible continuity, and so of personal identity.[3] It is hopeless for philosophical purposes to talk in vague terms of consciousness *feeling as if* it belonged together with other consciousness or of the *quality* of consciousness, and so on. Most importantly, since we are trying to offer an account of personal identity in terms of mental identity, rather than conversely, we must avoid all reference to 'parts of the same self', for such reference introduces a vicious circularity into the argument. Similar remarks apply to the notion of 'appropriation' on which James bases his analysis of sensible continuity. Appropriation is apparently an intentional relation between two experiences and, but for one crucial qualification, successful appropriation (i.e. appropriation of an experience which exists or existed) would appear to amount to remembering. The qualification, however, is that, whereas remembering is in no way a transitive relation, appropriation is transitive: if one experience appropriates a second, and the second a third, then the first appropriates the third. Indeed etymological considerations alone would suggest that in talking of 'appropriation' James is talking of 'parts of the same self', rather more briefly.[4]

However, the similarity between successful appropriation and successful remembering is sufficiently striking to encourage us to attempt in non-Jamesian terms an analysis of sensible continuity in terms of remembering. There are of course many different kinds of accusative for the verb 'remember': we can remember faces, people, places; arguments, theorems, rhymes, and quotations; how to tie a reef-knot, play the flute, embarrass Smith. We are not concerned with these cases, for none necessarily involves remembering *previous experiences* (previous encounters, previous learnings of arguments, previous tyings of reef-knots, and so on). We

---

[3] For an attempt to reconstruct James's account of personal identity, cf. A. J. Ayer, *The Origins of Pragmatism*, pp. 263–88.

[4] For the relation of appropriation, cf. James, op. cit. pp. 330–42.

are interested now solely in a fairly restricted set of memory-claims, namely claims to have had a certain experience at an earlier time ('I remember being annoyed at the time . . .', 'I remember the first time I opened "The Prelude" . . .', 'I remember learning Pythagoras' theorem . . .').

We can conveniently use the terminology which was used in discussion of qualitative continuity and the procedure will be very similar. The first stage is to define the 'R-relation': an experience cluster which includes what is remembered stands in R to the experience-cluster which includes the remembering. The second criterion of mental identity (namely sensible continuity), will then be as follows. The series S constitutes a single mind if it is possible to give a list of some of the members of S such that:

(i) the list is of pairs of members of S, the terms of each pair being related by R—let us call these R-pairs;

(ii) the R-pairs are arranged so that the first term of the first R-pair is the first member of S, and the second member of the last R-pair is the last member of S; and

(iii) the R-pairs are arranged so that the second term of each R-pair is also the first term of the succeeding R-pair (with the exception of the first term of the first R-pair and the last term of the last R-pair).

It is clear of course that the set of R-pairs will not necessarily be identical with the set of Q-pairs.

As soon as we begin to put pressure on the second criterion of mental identity devastating objections arise. Indeed it has all the weaknesses of the first criterion (weaknesses I shall not bother to rehearse again) together with a few of its own. It is clear that this account of sensible continuity (and so of mental identity) rests squarely on an account of memory, and that the account was intended to support a general claim that there is a very strong connection between mental and personal identity, a connection much stronger than the connection between bodily and personal identity. Reflection upon these considerations inspires two objections. The first is that I have talked quite wrongly of experiences as if they could be identified independently of their being located in, or with reference to, certain bodies. Both in identifying experiences and, more importantly, in checking memory-claims, I must fall back on a criterion of bodily identity. If a man claims to have watched a test-match at Lord's yesterday, I can check his claim only if I can determine whether a body resembling his in relevant respects was at Lord's yesterday in the appropriate place and attitude. So bodily identity through time is at the very least a necessary condition of mental identity through time.

In this form the objection is not particularly damaging, since it overlooks the distinction drawn earlier between two kinds of question, questions of classification and questions of reidentification, a distinction between, Is this object a person (rather than, say, a toffee-apple)? and, Is *this* person (at t_1) the same as *that* (at t_2)? It is certainly true, as I pointed out earlier, that we can identify experiences only as located in, or with reference to, a certain body at a certain time. To that extent the determination of mental identity presupposes successful identification of one or more bodies. But this is not to concede that there is any necessary connection between the identity of a particular body through time and the identity of a particular mind through time. As we saw in the discussion of the distinction between classification and reidentification, the formal procedure for deciding which series of all the possible series of experiences constitute particular minds is as follows. We identify a series as the series of experiences located in a certain body during a certain period. By applying various criteria of mental identity we discover whether that series constitutes a single mind, either on its own or together with another series, located in a different body at a different time; or whether parts of different such series together constitute a single mind, and so on. We locate our materials, as it were, by referring to bodies; thereafter we are free, if necessary, to rearrange them as seems most plausible, in accordance with the criteria of mental identity.

From the first objection, however, emerges a second, more damaging. The descriptivist has argued that bodily identity is only defeasibly necessary and defeasibly sufficient for personal identity, and that mental identity is sufficient (but not necessary) for personal identity. And the latest contribution to the account of mental identity—the analysis of sensible continuity—rests squarely on certain assumptions about memory. But in adopting this procedure he is guilty of a gross circularity. X and Y are the same person if S_x (one series of experiences) and S_y (another series of experiences) are sensibly continuous with each other; S_x and S_y are sensibly continuous with each other only if some member of

S_x stands in R to some member of S_y; in checking whether that relation holds we are checking whether a certain memory-claim is true; and strictly a memory-claim is true only if the person who claims to have done something did in fact do it. In short the account of mental identity presupposes a satisfactory account of personal identity. The circularity is vicious.

The only feasible reply to this objection increases rather than decreases our embarrassment, for it resurrects problems already partially solved. The general strategy is still to provide an account of mental identity in terms of sensible continuity. But the analysis of sensible continuity, while resting for all practical purposes on an account of memory, involves no formal reference either to memory or to personal identity and so avoids circularity. There are two features of memory which are crucial to the revised account of sensible continuity, features which (it is alleged) can be analysed without reference to personal identity. First, for an experience to be a memory-experience (of the kind we isolated earlier) it is necessary that it stand in a certain intentional relation to another, previous experience. Were it not for the danger of circularity, we might label this intentional relation 'ostensibly remembering'— 'ostensibly' because the previous experience may not exist, or other conditions of genuine remembering may not be fulfilled. Or we might borrow James's expression 'appropriation', with the important proviso, already stated, that appropriation for James is a transitive, almost one might say a cumulative, relation. For James, any experience-cluster which appropriates a previous one also appropriates those appropriated by the previous one, and so on. But if we are to talk of appropriation here, we must be taken as attempting to fabricate a non-tendentious label for ostensible memory.

So the first stage of the reply is to replace the R-relation in the account of sensible continuity by the rather weaker A-relation. The experience-cluster which includes what is remembered, we said, stands in R to the experience-cluster which contains the remembering. Correspondingly we can now say that the experience-cluster which contains what is appropriated (in the fabricated rather than full Jamesian sense of 'appropriate') stands in A to the experience-cluster which includes the relevant appropriating experience. All references to the R-relation will then be replaced by references to the A-relation in the formal statement of the criterion of sensible continuity.

The second stage involves drawing attention to the second crucial feature of memory, namely that for an 'appropriating' experience to be a genuine memory-experience it is necessary that the body in which (or with reference to which) it is located is the same body in which the previous 'appropriated' state was located. It is necessary because, as it happens, we stipulate that it is necessary. If I claim to have been in pain yesterday, and no pain-sensation was located in (or with reference to) my body yesterday, then I am simply mistaken. As we normally use 'remember' we have no use for a distinction between successful and unsuccessful appropriation. At very best the distinction can be taken as equivalent *either* to the distinction between appropriated experiences which exist and those which do not *or* to the distinction between appropriated experiences located in the same body as their corresponding appropriating states and those which are not.

So the second stage of the reply merely involves a slight elaboration of the revised criterion of sensible continuity: we stipulate that any two experiences related by A (an appropriating and an appropriated experience) must be located in (or with reference to) the same body. Thus the remembering relation is replaced by the appropriating relation; we have two conditions, severally necessary, jointly sufficient, for two experience-clusters' standing in the relation of appropriation; the reference to bodily continuity implicit in our notion of memory is retained, but there is no reference to memory as such. The general object of the manœuvre is to give an account of sensible continuity (for all practical philosophical purposes) in terms of memory, but without the circularity which follows inevitably from using the notion of memory itself.

The sceptical may accuse us of sophistry; they may suspect that the results are too good to be true, that they have been achieved only by logical sleight of hand, that the claim to have avoided vicious circularity is sincerely but mistakenly made. But there is no need for them to work back through the reply to the objection, to ask embarrassing questions about the notion of appropriation. I said that it avoided circularity only at the cost of reintroducing problems we had apparently partially solved. And even if we admit that the reply is a successful reply to the objection with which we were immediately concerned, it appears to provoke two devastating criticisms. First, it appears to vitiate the entire purpose of this chapter—and indeed the entire descriptivist enterprise. For the descriptivist drew attention (in Chapter 2) to certain striking facts about our notion of personal identity and argued that we should be strongly inclined to regard the criterion of mental identity as much more important than the criterion of bodily identity. In particular he drew attention to our inclination to describe the Bultitude case straightforwardly as a change-of-bodies case. But in the present state of play the only surviving account of mental identity is in terms of the criterion of sensible continuity; and in its revised form two experience-clusters are sensibly continuous only if they happen to be located in the same body. In short our desperate attempts to stop all loop-holes in the criterion of sensible continuity prevent us from describing the Bultitude case as a change-of-bodies case. According to the revised criterion of sensible continuity, the series of experiences in the February juvenile body cannot be sensibly continuous with the series in the March adult body, for the juvenile body is quite different from the adult body. Regarded from every point of view this is an acutely embarrassing result. Not merely does it commit us to an entirely counter-intuitive account of the Bultitude case, it also removes one of the main reasons for wanting to embark on a discussion of mental identity.

The second difficulty, or group of difficulties, is perhaps in these circumstances of less interest, but I shall point it out briefly before bringing this section to a close. It is precisely parallel to a difficulty encountered in the discussion of qualitative continuity. It was pointed out that qualitative continuity is not even sufficient for mental identity, let alone necessary. For to claim that qualitative continuity is sufficient for mental identity is to make no provision for those experiences which are qualitatively unique. Similarly the account of sensible continuity (whether in its original or in its revised form) makes no provision for experiences which neither appropriate nor are appropriated—or, as we would say, more loosely, for experiences which are neither (ostensible) remember-ings nor what are (ostensibly) remembered. Thus sensible con-tinuity cannot be sufficient for mental identity and, since it is clear that it cannot be necessary either (for a man may suffer complete amnesia while retaining very much the same kind of personality), the account of sensible continuity seems to have met with no more success than the account of qualitative continuity. As if this were not bad enough, we seem to be left with the problem of re-

duplication all over again. Just as there seemed no way of distinguishing between two qualitatively identical and temporally coincident series of experiences by means of the criterion of qualitative
continuity, so the criterion of sensible continuity offers us no way
of distinguishing between them. Indeed, as with the criterion of
qualitative continuity, we are rather invited to conflate any
number of such series into one series.

4. *Reduplication: a General Objection*

We might perhaps be tempted to begin the descriptive account
afresh, to adopt an entirely different approach. For it is clearly impossible to give a watertight account of mental identity in terms
either of qualitative or of sensible continuity, and there would
seem to be no alternative account available. It would be futile for
example to combine the two criteria, to argue that a series of
experience-clusters constitutes a single mind if parts of it are
qualitatively continuous, the other parts sensibly continuous, and
there are no simultaneous breaks in both qualitative and sensible
continuity. The move would be futile because the hybrid account
would be open to precisely those objections which undermined
each of the original accounts taken separately. We should be unable for example to make any provision for those experience-
clusters which were neither qualitatively unique nor sensibly
continuous with any other.

Moreover the problem of reduplication would still be very much
with us. And it is at this point that we may encounter a general
objection to the whole descriptivist enterprise, an objection which
brings the problem of reduplication to the centre of our attention.
The descriptivist has argued that mental identity is sufficient (but
not necessary) for personal identity, and that bodily identity is
defeasibly sufficient and defeasibly necessary for personal identity.
It is a consequence of this position that, in some cases at least, our
principle for counting persons will be dependent on our principle
for counting minds. In those cases therefore failure to supply a
general principle for counting minds is failure to supply a general
principle for counting persons.

The objection, from an orthodox Strawsonian position, is
simply that the descriptivist has failed to supply such a principle
for counting minds. He has failed to guarantee that, in locating
and identifying one mind, I am indeed identifying *one*, and not

two or twenty or two thousand. That is, he has failed to provide for the possibility that every series of experience-clusters is massively reduplicated, that there is a vast number of series S, S', S'', S''', . . . etc., all qualitatively indistinguishable, all temporally coincident, all located (if located at all) by reference to one body. The objection is emphatically not an invitation to revise our criteria of mental identity in such a way that the difficulty is resolved, the logical guarantee given. It is a general objection to all attempts to rest personal identity on some notion of mental identity (e.g. Cartesian and Humean accounts). The solution of the problem, it is suggested, is simple: it involves taking very seriously the claim that persons are logically prior to minds. That is, it involves interpreting the fourth thesis of the descriptivist account much more strongly than it has been interpreted so far. It is to be taken not merely as stating that the concept of a person cannot be analysed in terms of that of a mind; it is to be taken further as stating that the criteria of identity of persons cannot be dependent on the criteria of identity of minds. That is, it is suggested, the solution of our difficulties is to regard the principle for counting minds as dependent on the principle for counting persons, rather than the reverse:

The only way to guarantee a consequence which must surely rate as an adequacy condition for an admissible concept of an individual soul or consciousness—viz. that a normal man, in the course of a normal life, has at any time just one soul or consciousness which lasts him throughout—is to allow that the notions of singularity and identity of souls or consciousnesses are conceptually dependent on, conceptually derivative from, the notions of singularity and identity of men or people. The rule for deriving the criteria we need from the criteria we have is very simple. It is: *one* person, *one* consciousness; *same* person, *same* consciousness.[5]

The criteria we employ for counting persons will presumably vary from case to case. Standardly, bodily identity will be sufficient; in certain cases (e.g. the Bultitude case) we may decide to rely on criteria (however shaky) of qualitative or sensible continuity of a series of experiences. The logically prior task is to identify persons; the logically secondary task is to identify the minds or souls or consciousnesses which are ascribed to those persons.

I hope to show that although the objection is valid in its charge

[5] P. F. Strawson, *The Bounds of Sense*, pp. 168–9.

that the descriptivist has failed to offer a logical guarantee that a particular mind (and so a particular person) is not reduplicated, there is no reason to embrace the supposed solution of the difficulties with any enthusiasm. I shall try to show that such difficulties are common to all non-materialist accounts of personal identity (including Strawson's). The first stage of the reply is to note (yet again) that, given our cognitive apparatus, we can identify other people only as physical objects, as the possessors (in a broad, non-Cartesian sense of 'possessor') of certain bodies. If people were not material objects, did not have bodies, did not react physically either to their own condition, or to that of other things, did not talk, and so on, we should have no way of identifying others or the mental states of others.

For this reason among others[6] it is doubtful whether Strawson is entitled to entertain the hypothesis of (at least temporary) disembodiment.[7] However, it is quite clear that he can make sense of certain rather weaker cases. He points out for example that certain connections between a particular person and a particular body are contingent, that my vision may depend on the eyelids of one body, the position of a second, and the movement of the head of a third.[8] Presumably I could equally well express my thoughts from the lips of another body or raise another body's eyebrows, and so on. Suppose for example that three people, X, Y, and Z, all express their beliefs, memories, and feelings from the lips of Z's body. The situation might be confusing, but not logically incoherent. Of course, it will be pointed out, we should be able in that case to distinguish X, Y, and Z, because we should rapidly notice a systematic inconsistency in the avowals issuing from the lips of Z's body; a certain number would seem to form one group, others a second group, others a third. But let us suppose further (as, logically, we may) that X, Y, and Z have qualitatively identical experiences, at identical times, during the period in which we are interested. Given the general restrictions on the kinds of criteria we may use to identify persons, we have no way of distinguishing X, Y, and Z respectively. That is, an orthodox Strawsonian can offer no guarantee that a particular person (and so a particular

---

[6] For a thorough survey of the difficulties involved in the notion of disembodiment, cf. Penelhum's *Survival and Disembodied Existence*.

[7] *Individuals*, pp. 115–16.

[8] Ibid., pp. 90 f.

mind) is unique. His account and the descriptive account suffer from very similar difficulties: he cannot rule out the reduplication of persons and so cannot rule out the reduplication of minds; the descriptivist cannot rule out the reduplication of minds and so cannot rule out the reduplication of persons.

A *tu quoque* reply is rather unsatisfying. But if we investigate the *quoque* we see that the difficulties in which the descriptivist—and Strawson—are involved are common to all non-materialists. That is, they are shared by anyone who denies that personal identity and bodily identity are logically equivalent. It does not matter in the least whether one goes on to argue that bodily identity is necessary to personal identity, or whether one argues more radically that they are entirely independent of one another. As soon as one admits that there are non-physical criteria of personal identity one cannot avoid the problem of reduplication in some form or other.

Indeed one cannot avoid engaging in the general enterprise of this chapter. Criteria of personal identity do not work in a vacuum; they must involve the empirical identification of something or other; they must, as it were, have distinctive empirical *materials*. Where physical criteria of personal identity are inadequate (as in the case of identical twins) or useless (as in the Bultitude case) the only materials available to a non-materialist are experiences, identified in the ways I have sketched. But if he is to use these materials to formulate criteria of personal identity he must presumably attempt to pick out certain continuities in a series of experiences, continuities traditionally labelled continuities of character, of memory, continuities which I have tried to reduce to qualitative and/or sensible continuity. In short, anyone who wishes to deny that personal identity and bodily identity are logically equivalent—including Strawson—is committed to an enterprise essentially identical with the enterprise of this chapter. It does not matter whether we describe it (as Strawson would) as an attempt to formulate non-physical criteria of personal identity, or whether we describe it (as I have done) as an attempt to analyse mental identity. Every non-materialist is committed to making the attempt; however he describes what he is doing, the same problems arise, the same unresolved difficulties emerge; one is guilty of precisely the same failure, namely failing to give a watertight account of the non-physical criteria of personal identity.

Two questions now arise. First, we might ask, why should we persevere with the descriptivist approach of this chapter, rather than Strawson's orthodox alternative? Why should we continue to talk of 'mental identity' at all? Perhaps there are two reasons for the perseverance. The first, and less important, is that in talking of 'mental identity' one is implicitly stressing that, despite the close connection between persons and bodies, and between persons and minds, it is important to remember that persons, minds, and bodies are logically distinct—in the sense that the concept of a person cannot be exhaustively reduced to the concept of a mind or to the concept of a body or to any hybrid thereof. There can be personal continuity without bodily continuity and there can be personal continuity without mental continuity. Although a mind is necessarily someone's, it is important to remember that mental identity, though sufficient, is not necessary for personal identity, and it is helpful to keep them separate.

The second reason for continuing to talk of 'mental identity', for adopting the unorthodox approach of this chapter, is much more important. For if we reflect on the objection to that approach, made from Strawson's more orthodox position, and if we reflect on the reply to the objection, it becomes increasingly clear that there can be no orthodox approach to the problems of 'mental identity', so called. That is, if we suppose that the task is to give an account of the non-physical criteria of personal identity, and if we suppose that the only relevant materials available are series of experiences, then the orthodox proposal, that our principle for counting minds must be dependent on our principle for counting persons, involves a straightforward *hysteron proteron*. For if the application of non-physical criteria of personal identity involves the prior consideration of certain continuities or discontinuities in certain series of experiences, then the principle for counting minds will be logically prior to the principle for counting persons. The orthodox proposal overlooks the earlier distinction between problems of classification (Is this a person, or a table, or the illimitable Infinite, or $\sqrt{(-1)}$ . . . ?) and problems of reidentification (Is *this* person at t_0 the same as *that* at t_1 . . . ?). When solving a problem of classification we can certainly say, 'If there is *one* person here, there is one mind here.' But when solving a problem of reidentification, when applying non-physical criteria of personal identity through time, answers to questions about mental identity yield answers to questions about personal identity, rather than the reverse.

So much then for the first question provoked by the general comments on the need for an account of 'mental identity', that is of the non-physical criteria of personal identity. The second, and more embarrassing, question still remains, namely, how is the descriptivist to patch up the account he has offered in this chapter? The accounts both of qualitative and of sensible continuity floundered rapidly and convincingly because of their general failure to deal with more than a comparatively small range of cases. And even ignoring all the other difficulties of a more or less devastating kind, the problem of reduplication cropped up at every turn.

However, perhaps the time has come to be rather forthright over the problem of reduplication—after all, as has been pointed out, it is a problem common to any account of personal identity which involves reference to non-physical criteria of personal identity. We might dispose of the problem by stipulating that, unless a particular series of experiences exhibits a certain *systematic* inconsistency sufficient to support the claim that it is a compound series, formed from the experiences of more than one person, we are to assume that there is only one mind (and hence one person) to be identified. In a situation where in principle we have no way of deciding whether there is exactly one mind or two or twenty or two hundred, the request for a logical guarantee of uniqueness is entirely vacuous. When I cannot tell whether there is one mind or two or twenty or two hundred, it is at least in the interests of ontological economy that we stipulate that there is one and only one.

Ockham may dispose of one difficulty but it is not clear that he will offer any assistance with the others. It is unnecessary to rehearse again all the weaknesses afflicting the descriptive account of mental identity for they are all specific instances of a general weakness, a failure to make formal provision for all cases, both standard and deviant, that we are likely to encounter in discussion of personal identity. That is, they are all specific examples of a general failure to offer explicit and unequivocal criteria for resolving all disputes about personal identity. But perhaps the demand for *formal* provision, for *explicit* criteria, is misplaced; perhaps the best we can and should ask for is that the descriptivist make a series of *decisions* (of a fairly consistent and systematic kind) about the cases presented to him (ordinary cases, the Bultitude case, the Charles/Guy Fawkes case, and so on). I pointed out in the previous chapter how firmly descriptivism relies on our logical intuitions, on the descriptivist's general feeling that we *would* say such-and-such *if* circumstances were so-and-so. The revisionary metaphysician, as we shall see, prides himself on his precision; the descriptivist does not.

To demand decisions is of course not to demand *arbitrary* decisions. We may not expect a completely formal account of the criteria the descriptivist is using; we may only expect him to *decide* whether Charles is the same as Guy Fawkes, or whatever; but this is not to allow him to make arbitrary decisions. He will have reasons for his decisions and these reasons will involve substantial reference to the kinds of consideration which have inspired most of this chapter. For example the descriptivist may decide that two experiences are parts of the same series because they are apparently qualitatively continuous or because they are located in, or with reference to, the same body. He may decide that the Bultitude case is a genuine change-of-bodies case, because of certain apparent continuities between the experiences located in the February adult body, and those located in the March juvenile body, and vice versa. He may decide (as Williams does) that Charles and Guy Fawkes are not the same person, because of the radical break in bodily continuity. Or if he feels, somewhat heroically, that he can make sense of one person's being in two places at the same time, he may decide that Charles and Guy Fawkes and Robert are all the same person. In some of the most extraordinary cases I have mentioned, heroism may not sustain the effort; the circumstances are so peculiar that he may find it impossible to come to any decision at all.

In those cases in which decisions are made, however, we are entitled to ask for supporting reasons, although it may be unfair to demand a *general* account of all the reasons likely to be used in particular cases. This will mean among other things that the accounts of qualitative and sensible continuity will not be regarded as (putative) *formal* accounts of mental identity, but rather as suggestions, as guide-lines, as the sorts of reasons we might offer to support particular decisions on particular cases. 'Descriptive metaphysics is content to describe the actual structure of our thought about the world',[9] and 'the actual structure of our thought' is clearly often more pragmatic than systematic.

5. The Concept of Mind: a Second Objection

The descriptive account, warts and all, would seem to be virtually complete. In outline, it has gone like this: the descriptivist has argued that mental identity is sufficient (but not necessary) for personal identity, bodily identity defeasibly sufficient and defeasibly necessary. He has attempted to clarify mental identity in terms of the qualitative continuity of a series of experiences (or rather, more strictly, experience-clusters, groups of experiences) and then in terms of their sensible continuity. In both cases he failed; he could not give a watertight account of mental identity. However, it seemed clear that this embarrassment was by no means unique. Anyone who admits there are non-physical criteria of personal identity will be committed to a very similar enterprise, and will be involved in precisely similar difficulties. And however much we try to dress them up, the 'non-physical' criteria of personal identity will essentially be those of qualitative and sensible continuity. We may have to make decisions on personal identity, we shall have to support the decisions with reasons, and the reasons may well in some cases refer to qualitative and/or sensible continuity.

In reflecting on the enterprise of this and the previous chapter, however, we may become aware of another source of embarrassment. At the beginning of this chapter I noted in a rather offhand way that not all 'mental' activities could be analysed in terms of the occurrence of experiences, states of consciousness, and pointed out that the descriptivist is interested primarily in those activities which can be so analysed, that the materials of his inquiry are essentially those of Hume's account of personal identity. And we have therefore been examining the descriptivist's attempt to give an account of mental identity in terms of certain relations between (groups of) experiences. But it might reasonably be objected that this manœuvre should not be regarded as pardonable economy, but rather condemned as self-inflicted myopia; that it is absurd to offer an account of mental identity from which a large and by no means insignificant class of P-predicates is excluded. The point of offering an account of mental identity is to

9 P. F. Strawson, Individuals, p. 9.

illuminate the notion of personal identity without leaning on the notion of bodily identity. But the illumination is decidedly partial, if one concentrates on P-predicates which (implicitly or explicitly) ascribe particular experiences to someone. Indeed the source of the mistake is not hard to find. It is once again a failure to notice that the distinction between P- and M-predicates is not parallel to the traditionally understood distinction between 'mental' and 'physical'. An account of persons involves an analysis of P-predicates (of 'mental' predicates in a *very* broad sense) not of 'mental' predicates (in a narrow sense of 'mental').

It is very easy to find examples to support the objection. At least three connected groups of P-predicates immediately spring to mind. First, there is a group of action-predicates, such as 'is playing cricket', 'is driving to town', 'is teaching philosophy', 'is scratching his leg', etc. It is a philosophical commonplace (which, unlike certain other commonplaces, happens to be true) that many action-predicates cannot be analysed in terms of the occurrence of certain experiences, states of consciousness. The reason is partly that they may involve reference to human institutions, conventions, rules (and so an analysis in terms of the occurrence of experiences says too little); partly that they may not refer to the occurrence of any particular experiences at all (and so an analysis in terms of the occurrence of such experiences says too much); and partly that, although they are not M-predicates, they may refer essentially to some kind of physical activity. For example, if I am playing cricket I am involved in a rule-governed, conventional, or quasi-conventional activity; if I am scratching my leg I am not necessarily enjoying any particular kinds of experiences; and in both cases I am necessarily engaged in some kind of physical activity (batting, bowling, running about, scratching my leg).

Clearly such actions as playing cricket, teaching philosophy, even scratching one's leg, can be important in assessing whether X is the same person as Y. If X taught philosophy for twenty years and bowled vicious leg-breaks, for example, and Y is entirely ignorant of both philosophy and cricket, we are strongly inclined to conclude that X and Y are different people. Similar remarks apply to a second group of P-predicates, those ascribing general character-traits. We call a man an extrovert, not because he has particularly outward-looking or gregarious experiences but rather because he is at ease with other people, is not easily depressed, spends little time reflecting on the human condition in general and on his own in particular, and so on. Nor are there experiences characteristic of a careless man. Indeed his carelessness may sometimes be due to his persistent failure to have the right thoughts at the right time. At this point perhaps the second group of P-predicates overlaps with the third—those predicates ascribing intentions, or motives, or purposes, and those attributing responsibility. I can intend to be Prime Minister, be inspired by philanthropic motives, be entirely systematic and deliberate in everything I do, and be held responsible for my successes and failures, without having any particular experiences at any particular times. Of course, it might be said, it is at least a necessary condition of my significantly ascribing P-predicates of any of the three kinds to someone, that he is at least conscious. To use a rather archaic expression, he must be in *some* mode of consciousness, if not any *particular* mode. But this is clearly not so, and is seen not to be so as soon as we consider verbs of failure or verbs of refraining. I may fail to turn up, or deliberately refrain from turning up, for a class; and my failure or refraining may be achieved by my being fast asleep. Similarly, if I become drowsy at the wheel of my car and run someone down, I am blamed for negligence. The responsibility, the negligence, does not consist in my having certain experiences, but rather, one might say, in a failure to *perpetuate* my series of experiences.

It is not necessary to prolong the list of examples, for recent work in the philosophy of mind and philosophy of law is full of them. The main point is quite clear: some P-predicates do not, even in part, ascribe particular experiences, or experiences of a particular kind; some do not ascribe experiences at all; all, however, must be taken into consideration in an account of persons, for all ascribe properties which may be significant in disputes about personal identity. Perhaps another point is also clear (a point already mentioned in Chapter 2), namely that bodily identity is much more intimately connected with personal identity than the descriptivist has so far allowed. To say that the P-predicates under discussion ascribe properties of significance in settling disputes over personal identity is in effect to say that a man's physical size, shape, and efficiency, his facial expressions and bodily gestures, and so forth, will in part determine who he is. If X bowls vicious leg-breaks, sings over three octaves, smiles charmingly, and bites his nails, and Y does none of these things, I have a strong prima facie case for saying that X and Y are different people.

The points which together make up this rather long objection are of course substantially sound. But it is not quite clear what use the descriptivist is expected to make of them; it is not clear to what features of his account the objection is an objection. Two responses (at least) might commend themselves to him. First, he might regard it as an objection to the whole enterprise of resting personal identity so firmly on mental identity, interpreted as the identity of a series of experiences. According to this response, since persons perform actions, and since many actions cannot be analysed (either in part or, in some cases, at all) in terms of the occurrence of experiences, the Humean logical construction of the mind to which this chapter has been dedicated is fundamentally and irretrievably misguided. The moral to be drawn, perhaps, is that the materials with which we are confronted in dealing with the problem of personal identity are people's *states* in the broadest possible sense of the term—not merely their states of consciousness, but their actions, their physical states, their failings and refrainings. We should be looking for certain continuities between a man's states (in the broadest sense) rather than merely between his experiences, his states of consciousness.

It is a philosophically attractive response, since it tends to remove the beam in the eye of many empiricists, their tendency to regard people as essentially paralytic, the recipients of a constant stream of experiences, who never *do* anything. However, the descriptivist might prefer a second response. For in making the first he would not only commit himself to the very arduous task of providing a highly complex account of personal identity, he would do less than full justice to his original account. The second response consists in conceding everything the objector has to say but denying that the 'objection' is a genuine objection. To see the point of the response we must reflect on the general strategy of the descriptive account, the general point of giving mental identity such a prominent part in the account of personal identity. The aim has emphatically *not* been to *reduce* personal to mental identity in any important sense of that overworked word 'reduce'. The descriptivist can, and wishes to, claim that bodily identity is not only a criterion of personal identity, but sometimes a very important one, often for all practical purposes the only one. He cannot, and has no wish to, deny that a man's physical abilities and condition distinguish him from other men, that he could not engage in certain human activities without a body, and that he could not play his own characteristic part in those activities without his own body.

But 'all practical purposes' are not necessarily philosophically illuminating, and it is only by reflecting on rather peculiar cases that we gain philosophical understanding of concepts like that of a person. The descriptivist is merely putting pressure on the concept of a person to see whether certain criteria of personal identity are logically more important or more prominent than others. And as a result of applying such pressure he wishes to argue that there is a much more intimate connection between mental and personal identity than between bodily and personal identity. Both connections can be severed completely: the case of a man who changes character and suffers complete amnesia shows that mental and personal identity can be severed; the Bultitude case severs bodily from personal identity. But the Bultitude case also shows that the connection between mental and personal identity is rather more intimate than that between bodily and personal identity. There is a perfectly intelligible sense in which (falling back on the mental identity criterion) two people could be said to exchange bodies; there is no sense in which (falling back on the bodily identity criterion) they could be said to exchange minds. It may well be true (as the objector insists) that in making sense of changes of bodies we are concentrating to the exclusion of all else on P-predicates which ascribe states of consciousness. But the descriptivist would not want to argue that we are using our complete concept of a person, with all the trimmings, when we talk of changes of bodies. He merely wants to argue that, even bereft of all its trimmings, we still have something recognizable as our concept of a person and that therefore mental identity (in this narrow sense of 'mental') and personal identity are very intimately connected. He formally commemorates all these facts by insisting that while mental identity (interpreted narrowly) is sufficient for personal identity, bodily identity is *defeasibly* sufficient and *defeasibly* necessary for personal identity. And 'bodily' identity, presumably, will have to include all those physical similarities and continuities ascribed (directly or indirectly) by the sorts of P-predicates used as examples above.

6. The Descriptive Account: Final Observations

Since this chapter has been rather complicated, it might be useful to summarize the main points of the descriptive account. The fundamental claim is that the concept of a person is primitive, that people are neither essentially minds nor essentially bodies nor even combinations of both. There are, however, at least two kinds of criteria of personal identity, 'bodily' and 'mental', and the 'mental' criteria seem to occupy a very special position. That is, in putting pressure on the concept of a person, we can conceive of certain cases where the bodily criteria clearly break down, where apparent mental continuity is taken to be more significant than any bodily continuity. So the whole inquiry shifted (into another chapter) to the problem of making more detailed sense of mental identity or mental continuity. We tried to reduce mental identity to qualitative continuity and sensible continuity, but failed to produce a water-tight account. And, to make matters worse, it became clear that throughout the analysis we had been concentrating on a very small group of P-predicates, namely those ascribing states of consciousness. The only consolation was the thought that anyone who is not a materialist (or, perhaps, a radical behaviourist), anyone who wants to talk of non-physical criteria of personal identity, is committed to a similar enterprise and faces similar problems. The descriptivist has the satisfaction, then, of sharing difficulties with his non-materialist colleagues—although since he places such emphasis on mental identity his failure to produce a satisfactory analysis of it is rather more embarrassing than it would be to certain others.

Before moving on to the revisionary account I would like to draw attention to two features of the descriptive account which will become more prominent as the inquiry proceeds, and particularly prominent in Part IV. First, it was pointed out somewhat belatedly in this chapter that many of the predicates associated with the descriptivist concept of a person are action-predicates of one kind or another. Some of them refer to rather prosaic and logically simple actions (raising one's arm, smiling, assaulting, writing, and so on); some refer to rather more complex actions, to certain rules or conventions of human behaviour (signing a cheque, appealing in a law-court, taking out a marriage-licence, play-ing cricket, selling stocks and shares, and so on). And closely

connected with them are those predicates ascribing intentions, purposes, motives, reasons. All help, as it were, to give content to the
descriptivist concept of a person, and all are of crucial importance
to our inquiry, because, among other things, it is prima facie implausible to suggest that such predicates might be given a straightforward and complete physical interpretation. But that is to
anticipate.

Second, the basic items of the whole framework of which the
descriptivist concept of a person is a part are material objects
(including people) of a fairly large *macroscopic* kind. No attempt is
made (and no apology offered for failing) to refer to the minute
microscopic bits and pieces of which those bodies are composed.
In particular no attempt is made to relate or even to correlate
physical and mental states, save perhaps in the admission of
certain contingent causal connections between minds and bodies.
The sceptical might take the view that failure even to acknowledge
the facts of science exposes descriptivism as the expression of un-
informed and uninquisitive common sense; that, however much
we may reflect on the concepts implicit in our language, we have
no reason to suppose that they may not be revised to a greater or
lesser extent; and that the use of such concepts does not of itself
justify the use, unless reluctance to change our linguistic habits is
its justification.

Full examination of the advantages and weaknesses of the
descriptive account must wait until Part IV and we must be content to temper such scepticism for the moment with a single
thought, namely that the descriptive account is open to sceptical
attack principally because of its implicit acknowledgement of an
important empiricist principle, the principle that it makes sense to
talk of certain things only if it is possible to offer ways of identifying and reidentifying them. Our ability to identify anything at all
is a function of the efficiency of one or more of our senses. And in
comparison with microscopes, oscilloscopes, and so on, our senses
are rather primitive instruments, capable only of identifying
fairly chunky material objects. We might therefore regard the
descriptive account as (*inter alia*) expressing a certain kind of
limitation on our cognitive apparatus, a feature of our cognitive
constitution which is largely responsible for the prominence of
certain things as *basic* items in our everyday conceptual framework—namely material objects. The revisionary metaphysician, of

course, is of a rather more venturesome turn of mind and will take advantage of scientific instruments to pay more explicit attention to the microscopic structure of macroscopic objects. It is now time to investigate his endeavours and the concept of a person with which they appear to present us.

PART III

THE REVISIONARY ACCOUNT

'This is the first class in English spelling and philosophy, Nickleby', said Squeers, beckoning Nicholas to stand beside him.
'We'll get up a Latin one, and hand that over to you. Now, then, where's the first boy?'
'Please, Sir, he's cleaning the back parlour window', said the temporary head of the philosophical class.
'So he is, to be sure', rejoined Squeers. 'We go upon the practical mode of teaching, Nickleby; the regular education system. C-l-e-a-n, clean, verb active, to make bright, to scour. W-i-n, win, d-e-r, der, winder, a casement. When the boy knows this out of book, he goes and does it. It's just the same principle as the use of the globes. Where's the second boy?'
'Please, Sir, he's weeding the garden', replied a small voice.
'To be sure', said Squeers, by no means disconcerted. 'So he is. B-o-t, bot, t-i-n, tin, n-e-y, ney, bottiney, noun substantive, a knowledge of plants, he goes and knows them. That's our system, Nickleby; what do you think of it?'
'It's a very useful one, at any rate', answered Nicholas significantly.

(DICKENS, *Nicholas Nickleby*, Ch. VIII

4

SCIENCE AND PHILOSOPHY: MATERIALISM

1. *Two Kinds of Physicalism*

THE revisionary metaphysician would not perhaps regard the enterprise in which Squeers was engaged as a form of philosophical analysis. He would, however, heartily applaud the assumption on which it rested, namely that there is and must be a close connection between our philosophical beliefs and the discoveries of experimental science. He will be concerned to show that there is and must be a close connection between our analyses of certain concepts and the purely empirical facts revealed to us by the scientist. Scientific investigation will be expected to place certain limits on our everyday conceptual scheme and to influence the philosophical proposals we may make in attempting to analyse that scheme. To make any sense of the assumption we are probably best advised to treat it as essentially prescriptive. Save for periods in the seventeenth and twentieth centuries, it is doubtful whether philosophers have always been profoundly influenced by experimental science.

Indeed it would be improper to embrace the assumption shared by Squeers and the revisionary metaphysician, for to do so at this stage of the inquiry would be to beg the question against the descriptivist. I said (in Chapter 1) that revision presupposes something to revise and (in Chapter 3) that the descriptivist makes no reference, and offers no apologies for failing to refer, to the scientific facts about human beings. The onus of proof is on the revisionary metaphysician; he must prove that there *is* a close connection between scientific and philosophical proposals and that the descriptivist is at fault in neglecting it. So in formulating the physicalist thesis which is to constitute the revisionary account of the concept of a person we must keep the scientific and philosophical aspects of the inquiry quite separate. We must assume (at least until proof is offered to the contrary) that there is not one group of physicalist theses but two—those theses which will count as versions of *scientific* physicalism and those which will count as versions of *philosophical* physicalism. In general scientific physicalism will consist in the claim that all organic phenomena can be scientifically explained and predicted in terms of those concepts and laws which serve to explain and predict inorganic phenomena, i.e. the concepts and laws of physics. Philosophical physicalism on the other hand will consist in the claim that any coherent statement about an organic individual can be reduced to a statement or set of statements about inorganic individuals, that is, to statements about the primitive individuals of physics.

It is only fair to point out that many (philosophical) physicalists talk as if the distinction were spurious. Armstrong for example says:

[The object of this book] is to show that there are no good philosophical reasons for denying that mental processes are purely physical processes in the central nervous system and so, by implication, that there are no good philosophical reasons for denying that man is nothing but a material object.

It does not attempt to prove the truth of this physicalist thesis about the mind. The proof must come, if it does come, from science: from neurophysiology in particular.[1]

To suggest that the proof of the philosophical thesis must come from science is in effect to overlook the distinction between scientific and philosophical physicalism. That the oversight is unfortunate is surely clear. The adoption or rejection of scientific physicalism depends on the acquisition of empirical evidence about certain kinds of correlation between events; the adoption or rejection of philosophical physicalism will not depend (at least, by no means entirely) on the acquisition of empirical evidence. It is only by reflecting on the ways in which we commonly use certain concepts, and in particular on our reasons for needing them, that we can decide whether they should be revised (or even discarded) to accommodate the discoveries of physical science. In short it is possible and in no way perverse to accept scientific and to reject philosophical physicalism.

It is neither unfair nor misleading to characterize the conflict between the descriptive and revisionary metaphysician in terms simply of their respective attitudes to the two physicalist theses I

---

[1] D. M. Armstrong, *A Materialist Theory of the Mind*, p. 2.

have distinguished. As the comment from Armstrong would suggest, the revisionary metaphysician is attempting as far as possible to conflate the two theses, to show that if we can explain and predict all organic phenomena in terms of the concepts of physics then we should be prepared to analyse all statements about organic phenomena in precisely the same way. This attempt will be the topic of Part III. The descriptivist, on the other hand, is concerned at all costs to resist the conflation, to offer reasons for rejecting philosophical physicalism whatever our attitude to scientific physicalism may be. We shall be contemplating his efforts in Part IV. We must now begin our examination of the revisionary account. In this chapter I shall sketch the scientific assumptions of philosophical physicalism and expound one philosophical thesis which such scientific assumptions are supposed to support. I shall point out its defects and in the next chapter will offer a rather more promising alternative, which we shall take to be the most serious revisionary threat to the descriptive account of persons offered in Part II.

2. *From Correspondence to Identity*

Let us turn therefore to the first stage of the revisionary account, the initial scientific assumptions. Although scientific information about the activities of organisms in general and of human beings in particular is still relatively limited, two assumptions may be made at once. First, we may assume that all experiences, states of consciousness, may be explained in physical terms, 'explained' in the sense that (i) any such state may be described as a function of (the values of) certain variables, namely the primitive variables of physics and (ii) given a sufficiently comprehensive state-description in physical terms of an organism at a given time, it is in principle possible to predict the occurrence of all the immediately subsequent states of the organism, including its states of consciousness.

Second, we may assume that the concepts and laws of biology, psychology, and even chemistry can in principle be reduced to the concepts and laws of physics. The biological, psychological, and chemical properties of an organism can in principle be reduced to its physical properties. Since we are to be fairly frequently embarrassed by the word 'reduce' and its cognates, it is important that we make quite clear the sense in which we are using it here.

Clearly the 'reduction' to the concepts and laws of physics is not a *logical* reduction, of the kind we refer to when we say that the properties of a polygon may be reduced to the properties (including relational properties) of its parts. For we want to say that the connection between the properties of the polygon and the properties of its parts is a logically necessary connection, that we may validly *deduce* the properties of the whole from the properties of the parts. In contrast, the chemical, psychological, and biological properties of an organism are only *contingently* connected with its physical properties. So when we say that all scientific concepts and laws can be reduced to those of physics, we mean that physics can furnish us with a set of concepts and laws which will fulfil all our explanatory and predictive purposes as efficiently as the concepts and laws of, say, biology, psychology, and chemistry.

I see no point in challenging this account of the ideal of a comprehensive and unified science. As will become clear in Part IV, it is by no means the purely scientific assumptions of the revisionary account which provoke the philosophically crucial problems, which are responsible for the weaknesses in the revisionary account. For our philosophical purposes the assumption that scientific physicalism is true is important, not for any claims it may appear to support about the nature, extent, and future development of scientific investigations but rather as an essential preliminary to the philosophical inquiry. Only in the event of there being a radical revision of the concepts and laws of physics, or of its being found more expedient to 'reduce' all scientific laws to those of, say, chemistry rather than physics, would any significant philosophical difficulties arise from the assumption.

Let us therefore suppose that the ideal of a unified science will indeed be attained in the way the physicalist suggests, and move on to the next stage of the argument. The physicalist or revisionary metaphysician is concerned to give an account of those individuals in which we are interested—namely persons—in terms which implicitly concede as much as is philosophically permissible to the discoveries of physical science. Or more crudely, as I pointed out earlier, he wishes, as far as is philosophically possible, to conflate scientific and philosophical physicalism. The two scientific assumptions we have just made amount to a version of scientific physicalism but they leave open all the philosophical issues. All that has been claimed (and conceded) so far is that any given experience (state of consciousness) can be described (and in principle predicted) as a function of certain purely physical states or processes. That is, we have conceded the truth of a fairly weak scientific hypothesis which has been labelled, and which I shall continue to refer to as, the *Correspondence Hypothesis*, the hypothesis that an experience of a certain (specifiable) kind will occur if and only if a physical state (or states) of a certain (specifiable) kind occurs.

Strictly of course it is more of a model of Correspondence Hypotheses, than a Correspondence Hypothesis, for there will be as many such hypotheses as kinds of experience. There will be one correlating pains in the left foot with one kind of physical state, another correlating pains in the back of the head with another kind of physical state, another correlating thoughts about Ramsay MacDonald with yet another kind of physical state, and so on. So references to 'the Correspondence Hypothesis' must be taken as shorthand for references to the very large number of specific hypotheses correlating specific kinds of experience with specific kinds of physical state. But this is, I should have thought, a very obvious and somewhat peripheral complication which will not affect the course of the argument.

I said that the philosophical problems remain: the Correspondence Hypothesis does not commit us to any specific account of the connection between experience and physical states. There is still a further step to be made to the much stronger claim that here we have not merely correspondence but *identity*—the claim which the physicalist wants to make. It is absolutely vital to emphasize, as some physicalists [2] are wont to forget, that this step is indeed a *step*, requiring justification. As the Correspondence Hypothesis stands it is compatible not merely with the Identity Theory (that experiences are identical with certain physical states, notably those of the brain and nervous system); it is also compatible with the two most popular alternative theories of mind, Interactionism (whether in a Cartesian or weaker form) and Epiphenomenalism. All three theories enable us to explain and predict the occurrence of no more and no fewer experiences than can be scientifically noted, and all three offer an explanation of the precise connection between experiences and physical states.

[2] But not J. J. C. Smart, in his *Philosophy and Scientific Realism*, pp. 11 ff., from which the argument immediately following is drawn.

However, in moving from the Correspondence Hypothesis to the Identity Theory, rather than to a version of Interactionism or to Epiphenomenalism, the physicalist will emphasize three desiderata, the explanations each theory affords, the ontological claims of each theory, and the role of such ontological claims in those explanations. And he will stress the advantages of a judicious use of Ockham's razor, since there is presumably no very good reason for introducing metaphysical hypotheses to perform functions already perfectly well performed by other less ambitious hypotheses. If we allow the virtues of an Ockhamist approach to impress themselves upon us (he will argue) it becomes clear that the Identity Theory is by far the simplest, for it alone postulates only one kind of thing in giving content to the Correspondence Hypothesis. In comparison the other alternatives seem excessively complicated. All forms of Interactionism and Epiphenomenalism involve postulating *two* kinds of thing, physical states and experiences (or in the case of Cartesian Interactionism, physical and mental substances); both therefore also demand a set of psychophysical laws, relating the two kinds of thing. Since the Identity Theorist has only one kind of entity to start with, he is apparently not compelled to offer any account of the relation between physical states and experiences. The 'relation' is that of identity.

3. *Initial Formulation of the Identity Theory*

So much then for the first main step in the physicalist's argument, the move from the Correspondence Hypothesis to the Identity Theory, with Ockham as our guide. The facility of the move should not, I think, disturb us; a certain measure of philosophical economy is to be welcomed rather than eschewed. The major problem still remains, that of formulating the Identity Theory correctly. First, a few introductory observations which will give us a general grasp of what the Identity Theory is all about. Given the resources of our language (which for the moment is the only language available to the Identity Theorist), we can in principle offer two categorially distinct accounts of what is happening when a state of consciousness, an experience, occurs. Whether they count as accounts of the *same* events will, of course, depend on our theory of mind: the Interactionist and Epiphenomenalist will want to treat them as different, the Identity Theorist as the *same*, events. Thus we can offer a 'phenomenal' account ('I am suffering from toothache'); or we can describe a certain number of the physical properties of a certain brain and nervous system at a certain time ('There is a softening of the core of the tooth as the result of decay, leading to stimulation of an adjacent nerve-ending . . . etc.'). The Identity Theorist claims that the singular term ('toothache') in the 'phenomenal' description refers to the *same* thing as the singular term or terms ('softening', 'stimulation', . . .) in the 'physical' description, that the mental state described by the first is identical with the physical state or states described by the second. A flash of lightning, he reminds us, is *in fact* identical with an electrical discharge in the atmosphere; the sound of an A is *in fact* identical with vibrations of the air of 440 c.p.s.; similarly, my toothache is *in fact* identical with certain complex states of my tooth, brain, and nervous system.

There are two features of this general outline of the Identity Theory which should give pause for thought—the notion of identity, and the notion of a state, or process, or event. Let us first pause with the notion of identity. Standard formulations of the Identity Theory ('pains are identical with brain-processes', and so forth), apart from doing violence to our linguistic intuitions, obscure vital and fundamental features of the notion of identity. They also, it would seem, encourage philosophers to toy with entirely spurious distinctions between 'strict' and 'theoretical' identity. Identity does not admit of degrees or variations; a thing is neither strictly nor theoretically identical with something else; it is simply identical with it or not, as the case may be. Perhaps the temptation to think otherwise is in part due to forgetting that if two singular terms refer to the same thing, then we do indeed have but *one* thing.

Perhaps a rather more sophisticated way of making the same point is to say that, if two things are identical, then they are identical *under a certain description*, where the description offers a principle of counting. In Chapter 1 I drew attention to those general terms (such as 'cat', 'bottle', 'person') which yield a principle of counting and those (such as 'red', 'wet', 'soft') which do not. Clearly, if we are concerned to pick out certain things as identical with others *under a certain description*, the descriptions must be of the first kind rather than the second. So it is a trifle misleading to say that experiences are *in fact* identical with physical states: if we have a suitable description which can appropriately be applied to both, then they are identical; if not, not. In formulating the Identity Theory, therefore, we are not providing some kind of empirical answer to the empirical question, How many things are there?, but rather providing an answer to the question, How many things should we distinguish? Further, we expect the theory to provide an answer to the question, Under what description or kinds of description are experiences and physical states identical? Are they for example identical under a 'physical' description or under a 'phenomenal' description?

The second problem which should give us pause for thought concerns the expressions '*state* of consciousness', 'brain-*state*', 'brain-*process*', 'mental or physical *event*'. Not merely does their use invite rather than eradicate confusion, it is curiously inconsistent with the Ockhamist principles of the Identity Theorist. For if we reflect on the logical status of brain-*states* or brain-*processes*, we realize that they are essentially secondary particulars, constructed from the properties of a brain and nervous system; and *states* of consciousness are similarly logical constructions from the properties of the persons or organisms whose states they are. As such they are redundant. Let us consider brain-states first. Let us suppose that P_1, P_2, . . . etc. are bits of a particular brain and nervous system (what we shall call 'brain-parts'); and suppose that the following propositions are true:

    (i) P_1 is discoloured, at t.

    (ii) P_2 has an electrical potential of such-and-such, at t.

P_1 and P_2 are our primary particulars, but we can if we wish construct two secondary particulars, namely the discoloration of P_1, and the possession of P_2 of an electrical potential of such-and-such. The secondary, constructed, particulars are brain-*states*, or brain *processes*.

Similarly, states of consciousness, experiences, are secondary particulars, constructed from the properties of certain primary particulars, namely persons. Instead of saying that Jones is thinking at t, I can talk of Jones's *thought*; instead of saying that Smith is perceiving something at t, I can talk of Smith's *perception*; and so on. Just as we may expect the physicalist to be reluctant to talk of brain-states or processes when he can talk more economically of the properties of brain-parts, parts of a brain and nervous system, so we may expect him to be reluctant to talk about states of consciousness when he can talk about the properties of some relevant primary particulars. However, impressed as he is by the Correspondence Hypothesis, it is unlikely that the 'relevant primary particulars' will be persons. It is more natural for him to try to reduce states of consciousness to the 'phenomenal' properties of brain-parts. His Identity Theory will in turn be a theory about the possession by brain-parts of both 'physical' (or, for short, ϕ-)properties, and 'phenomenal' (or, for short, ψ-)properties.

These reflections on the notion of a state or process suggest ways of resolving both the naïve and the sophisticated worries about the notion of identity. If we ask the naïve question, To what *one* thing do a given 'physical' description and the corresponding 'phenomenal' description refer?, we may answer, A brain-part, a part of a brain and nervous system. And if we ask the more sophisticated question, Under what description are a given brain-state and its corresponding experience identical?, we answer, Under the description 'Such-and-such a brain-part'. And we are then in a position to state the Identity Theory, the fundamental thesis of the revisionary account. Let us state it as follows: there is a certain sub-set of physical particulars, namely brain-parts, parts of a human brain and nervous system. Each brain-part has two kinds of properties: on the one hand, it can be described as having spatial and temporal extent, as being coloured, as having a certain electrical potential, and so on—these are 'physical' or ϕ-properties; on the other hand, it can be described as pain-ish, or red-sense-impression-ish, or thought-about-Napoleon-ish—these are 'phenomenal' or ψ-properties. The ψ-properties of brain-parts will be known only by introspection, and introspection, we may presume, will be interpreted as consisting in the 'scanning' of one brain-part by another in the way suggested by Armstrong: 'In perception the brain scans the environment. In awareness of the perception another process in the brain scans that scanning.'[3] The ϕ-properties of brain-parts, on the other hand, can be known only by physiological inspection.

One point needs to be emphasized, and will be of such importance in what follows that I shall dignify it with the title, the *Contingency Thesis*. The Identity Theorist wishes to insist that the connection between physical states, notably brain-states, and experiences is logically *contingent*; indeed the scientific investigation which yielded the original Correspondence Hypothesis

[3] D. M. Armstrong, op. cit., p. 94.

would be entirely out of place were the connection not contingent. Thus, it is logically possible that a certain (specifiable) brain-state, which is in fact identical with a pain-experience, might have been identical with a red sense impression, or a thought about Ramsay MacDonald; and, more radically, it is logically possible that heart-states or liver-states or spleen-states or appendix-states, rather than brain-states, might be identical with experiences. Translating from the language of brain-*states* into the language of brain-*parts* and their properties, the Contingency Thesis consists in the claim that it is entirely contingent that any brain-part (i.e. any part of a human brain and nervous system), described in terms of its physical, or ϕ, properties, has certain phenomenal, or ψ-, properties. It is logically possible that a certain brain-part which is, say, pain-experience-ish, might have been, say, thought-about-Ramsay-MacDonald-ish; and, more radically, it is also logically possible that liver-parts or spleen-parts or appendix-parts or heart-parts, rather than brain-parts, might have phenomenal, or ψ-, properties.

Before closing this section three clarificatory points might be made. First, we might feel a certain uneasiness over the introduction of phenomenal or ψ-properties; we might find it a trifle disturbing to talk of a brain-part as pain-ish or green-sense-impression-ish or whatever. But as we have seen from the discussion of states and processes, of their ontological redundance, the physicalist has no alternative but to introduce these somewhat unwieldy properties. He does not wish to introduce any more *kinds* of individual than are necessary to his enterprise. He can, he thinks, express everything he wishes to express, as a result of his scientific investigations, in terms of the (ϕ- or ψ-) properties of a certain kind of primary particular, the brain-part. He is therefore forced to discard our ordinary range of expressions referring to experiences, states of consciousness, in favour of a new, rather unfamiliar, rather unwieldy, set—but he can hardly be expected to regard that as a disadvantage. (One might wonder, perhaps, whether a dualism of properties represents any advance upon a dualism of things; but I shall not pursue the point.)

Second, we are not committed at the moment to any particular analysis of ψ-properties; nor are we committed to any particular view about the status in the physicalist framework of what might be called the *phenomenal content* of experiences. These are obscurities to be eradicated in the course of this and the following chapter. Third, the Identity Theory is not a strict translatability theory. That is, the Identity Theorist may point out with perfect consistency that, given the present category-differences of our language, 'physical' and 'phenomenal' individuals are of different kinds and that statements about experiences cannot be translated into statements about physical individuals. As we have already observed, he may be expected to recommend that certain linguistic reforms be made. So far the reforms have only extended to the replacement of certain P-predicates (ascribed to persons) by certain ψ-predicates (ascribed to brain-parts), but as his argument continues the reforms will become steadily more far-reaching.

4. *Phenomenal Properties and Contingency* (1)
Having formulated the Identity Theory, it would be very gratifying to be able to move on to the evaluation of the competing claims of the descriptive and revisionary accounts. Unfortunately the gratification must be postponed. Not only is it necessary to formulate the complete revisionary account, of which the Identity Theory is merely the nucleus; there are more immediate difficulties to be resolved, which arise from our introducing phenomenal or ψ-properties, and which will occupy us for the rest of this chapter and for most of the following chapter. We must try to explain the status of ψ-properties and to explain in what respects they differ from 'physical' or φ-properties. The only pertinent comment I have made so far is that ψ-properties are known (directly) only by introspection, φ-properties by physiological examination, but this comment provokes at least two questions. First we might ask, What exactly is being introspected when ψ-properties are identified by introspection? And, second, we might ask whether ψ-properties are genuine *properties* of brain-parts, whether they can be accommodated in a physicalist account of persons.

The first question is an important one precisely because it has been denied that there are any introspectible phenomenal properties. The dispute does not really centre on 'introspectible', for, as we have seen, physicalists are prepared to make a shot at offering an entirely physicalist account of introspection, as the scanning of one part of the brain by another. It centres rather on the expression 'phenomenal' and the denial is a denial that there are any things or properties which are not physical (or ϕ-ish) things or physical (or ϕ-) properties. For example J. J. C. Smart says: 'I am ... denying that we introspect any nonphysical property such as *achiness*. To say a process is an ache is simply to classify it with other processes that are felt to be like it, and this class of processes constitutes the aches.'[4] It would be inappropriate to investigate his non-philosophical motives for denying that there are any introspectible phenomenal properties. We may suppose that he sincerely believes that there are not. But one important philosophical motive is clearly his belief that to talk of 'any non-physical property such as achiness' involves introducing 'emergent' properties and 'emergent' psycho-physical laws, properties and laws which cannot be deduced from the properties and laws of physics: 'These considerations turn upon the seeming impossibility of fitting these *qualia*, in any plausible way, into the body of our scientific knowledge. . . . There would have to be special irreducible laws which relate the complex neurophysiological processes to the corresponding sense-data.'[5] In this passage Smart is reflecting specifically on the status of so-called sense-data ('qualia') of the secondary qualities, but his argument is a general objection against any attempts to add to the neurophysiological story an account of irreducible phenomenal occurrences.

I wish to show that he is entirely misguided, that there are introspectible phenomenal properties, that indeed he must admit their existence, and that such prima facie non-physical properties can be accommodated within physicalism without too much embarrassment. As an initial amateur exercise in phenomenology, we might indicate what ψ-properties are supposed to be. In general an experience has phenomenal content in so far as it enters consciousness at all, in so far as it is a state of consciousness. To use the rather outmoded distinction between determinables and determinates, phenomenal properties will be determinates of the determinable property *being a state of consciousness*. It is the determinate phenomenal content of an experience which will distinguish it from other experiences. The particular phenomenal content of an experience of pain is that which makes it an experience of pain, not of heat, or tickling; it is that which makes a visual experience a perception of a red expanse, not a yellow or a

4 J. J. C. Smart, 'Materialism', pp. 654–5.
5 Id., *Philosophy and Scientific Realism*, p. 68.

blue; it is that which makes an auditory experience a perception of the sequence A, C, D, and not, say, B, D, G. (In all these cases, of course, we should strictly translate from the language of states or experiences to the language of brain-parts and their ψ-properties.)

Clearly we must tread rather warily here, for not all so-called 'states of consciousness' will have very distinct determinate ψ-properties, distinct phenomenal content. Physical sensations and all the clockable experiences peculiar to each sense will have a very distinctive phenomenal content; certain states (thinking about a problem, day-dreaming) will be rather less clear cases; and certain general states (depression, 'a general feeling of well-being', amusement, disappointment, annoyance) can reasonably be said to have very little introspectible phenomenal content. This point incidentally is not to be confused with the point I made in Chapter 2, that not all mental activities involve the occurrence of states of consciousness. But, of course, the greater our reluctance to identify appropriate states of consciousness, the greater our reluctance to identify any determinate phenomenal content.

To suppose that these reflections can have any force against Smart's position is to be guilty of a degree of optimism quite alien to the inquiry. At best these variations on the theme of phenomenal content serve to fill in certain details of the revisionary account; at worst they do not advance the argument at all. To show the weaknesses of Smart's position we must go rather more indirectly to work. First, we might, with a certain amount of philosophical self-indulgence, resort to an *ad hominem* argument of the kind which Feigl presents against the 'tough-minded' materialist: 'Don't you want anaesthesia if the surgeon is to operate on you? And if so, what you want prevented is the occurrence of the (very!) raw feels of pain, is it not?'[6] It would seem entirely pointless to ask for an anaesthetic, if one supposed merely that it would inhibit a certain set of (non-introspectible) physical responses; similarly it is odd to suppose that I refrain from putting my hand into a fire merely because I am reluctant to go red in the face, dance around the room, and so on. Certainly reference to all these responses to stimuli will occur in a comprehensive account of my visit to the hospital or my burning myself, but to suppose that they are the *only* relevant features of the account is

[6] H. Feigl, *The 'Mental' and the 'Physical'*, p. 390 (reprint, p. 23).

entirely wrong. We want to say that a highly relevant feature of the account is a reference to the 'raw feel', the 'phenomenal content' peculiar to an experience of pain. We want to say that we ask for an anaesthetic because surgical probings of our body *hurt*, that we withdraw our hand from the fire because the fire *burns*, gives us painful sensations, that these sensations of pain are logically quite independent of the sort of non-introspective physical response in which Smart appears to be interested.

This first, *ad hominem*, point is by no means conclusive. Smart can insist, implausibly but consistently, that in avoiding painful sensations I *am* (and am only) trying to inhibit a series of physical responses, overt or otherwise. We must turn to a more complicated argument which shows conclusively that the rejection of phenomenal properties involves him in incoherence. Consider Smart's analysis of our ordinary experience-reports, for example (to use one of his examples) his analysis of 'it looks to me that there is a yellow lemon'. His suggested analysis is, 'what is going on in me is what goes on in me when there really is a yellow lemon in front of me, my eyes are open, the light is daylight, and so on.'[7] He realizes of course that difficulties might arise if we put pressure on the expression 'yellow lemon' and makes it clear that his analysis is to be interpreted in the light of his more general thesis about the identity of experiences and brain-processes. He wants us to conceive of experience-reports as essentially *classifications*, classifications of experiences as like/unlike other experiences. So in saying that there seems to be a yellow lemon in front of me I am not reporting any phenomenal occurrences at all; I am simply and solely claiming that what is going on in me at *t* (whatever it might be) is like what went on in me at *t*-1 (when there was a yellow lemon in front of me, in daylight . . . etc.), and is unlike what went on in me at *t*-2 (when there was an orange in front of me, or a white elephant . . . etc.).

Of course it is objected that one cannot say that two things are alike unless one can in principle specify in what respect they are alike. One cannot say that two experiences are similar or dissimilar unless one can say in what respect they are similar or dissimilar. But Smart rejects the objection out of hand, for, he argues, the respect in which two experiences are similar or dissimilar is the similarity or dissimilarity between the brain-states

[7] J. J. C. Smart, 'Materialism', p. 654.

with which they are identical. We can certainly say that two experiences are similar or dissimilar, because we have them. We cannot specify the respect in which they are similar or dissimilar because we do not have the relevant physiological information available. He invites us to consider a machine which is built to distinguish round, square, and triangular discs, and he points out that it would be easier to construct a machine that would simply divide the discs into groups than it would be to construct a machine that told us the principle of division.[8]

It is not at all clear that this example proves anything at all. Indeed it may serve to confirm the suspicion of Smart's opponents that he is ignoring the crucial difference between artificial machines and the human machine. Whereas Smart's machine can only divide discs into groups without being aware of the principle of division, the human machine *is* aware of the principle of division. It is certainly true that it is easier to build a machine which can perform merely the simple activity (of dividing into groups) than to build one which can perform the more sophisticated (of articulating the differences between the groups). But it is still true that the human machine is capable of both kinds of activity.

It is tempting to press the attack on Smart even further, to argue that his analysis of experience-reports is circular, that if we say merely that e_1 is like e_2, we must either say in what respect it is like e_2 or we must say that e_2 is like e_3, which is like e_4, which is . . ., which is like e_n, which is like e_1. Unless we classify experiences in terms of their phenomenal content, the whole operation of classifying them as like/unlike others is not only wholly arbitrary but logically vicious. But Smart is (at least temporarily) on strong ground, for a reason I have just mentioned. Since experiences are *in fact* brain-processes, he will say, a certain experience is like/unlike another in virtue of a certain brain-process's being like/unlike another. One can know that an experience is like/unlike another without knowing in what respects they are like/unlike, for one does not have available the relevant physiological information to determine in what respects they are like/unlike.

But Smart invites a much more damaging objection. As I pointed out earlier, an essential feature of the Identity Theory is

[8] Ibid., p. 655.

the claim that the identity of experiences and brain-processes is *contingent:* 'Were the scientific facts otherwise we might have had to identify experiences with heart processes or liver processes, for example.'[9] An important and conclusive objection can be formulated to show that by eliminating all reference to ψ-properties Smart is committed to rejecting the Contingency Thesis. To highlight the main stages of the objection it might be useful first to consider an analogy: suppose, for scientific reasons, it is legitimate to describe a man in no more than two ways. The first description is 'the individual similar to Jones, Brown, and White', the second is 'the first man to climb Mt. Everest'. And suppose we want to make a contingent identity-statement of the general form: 'Smith = the first man to climb Mt. Everest.' The first description cannot usefully be substituted for 'Smith' because it is implicitly circular. By adopting the same procedure in the case of Jones, Brown, and White, we should eventually arrive at a statement of the form: 'That (i.e. Smith) which is like Jones, who is like Brown, who is like White, who . . ., who is like Smith = the first man to climb Mt. Everest.' To articulate an identity-statement at all, we must use *identifying* expressions, and an entirely circular characterization of Smith will not count as an *identifying* expression. So we cannot hope to articulate our identity-statement by describing Smith in the first way.

Unfortunately it also appears that we cannot resort to the second description either. For if we describe Smith as the first man to climb Mt. Everest, the only pertinent identity-statement which can be formulated is the statement: 'The first man to climb Mt. Everest = the first man to climb Mt. Everest.' And this statement is necessary (an instance of $(x)(x = x)$) not contingent. It may well be contingent that the first man to climb Mt. Everest is the first man to climb Mt. Everest, where the 'is' is the 'is' of predication, for he might well have never climbed Mt. Everest at all. But it is logically necessary that the first man to climb Mt. Everest is *identical* with the first man to climb Mt. Everest.

The force of the example rests of course on the (correct) assumption that the necessity or contingency of statements is a function of the kinds of description employed in them. If we keep this assumption firmly in mind, and if we apply the analogy to Smart's analysis of the relation between experiences and brain-

[9] J. J. C. Smart, *Philosophy and Scientific Realism*, p. 101.

processes, we see quite clearly that his position is incoherent. He is concerned to formulate contingent identity-statements of the form: 'My (apparently) perceiving a yellow lemon at t = certain brain-processes at t.' The individual (or set of individuals) referred to on each side of the '=' sign is referred to in two different ways—as the (apparent) perception of a yellow lemon at t, and as certain brain-processes at t. If we are, with Smart, to regard experience-reports as classifications, we must analyse 'My (apparently) perceiving a yellow lemon at t' as 'The experience at t, like the experiences at t_1, t_2, unlike the experiences at t_3, t_4 . . .' But as the analysis stands we are left with an entirely uninformative, entirely circular, characterization of the (apparent) perception of a yellow lemon, namely as the experience at t which is like that at t_1, which . . ., which is like the experience at t.

As I have already observed, each term of an identity-statement must consist of an identifying expression if the identity-statement is to be articulated at all. It is worse than pointless, it is incoherent, to attempt to articulate an identity-statement one of whose terms does not purport to identify an individual. For this reason an entirely circular characterization of an (apparent) perception of a yellow lemon at t cannot be admitted as a term in a (putative) identity-statement; it is not an *identifying* description at all. Presumably, if we ask Smart to offer an alternative analysis of 'the (apparent) perception of a yellow lemon at t', he will suggest something of the form 'the experience at t which is identical with certain brain-processes at t' (in the way that our hypothetical scientist above suggested something of the form 'the first man to climb Mt. Everest'). Unfortunately for Smart's purposes the suggestion is disastrous. If the only non-circular characterization of an experience is to be in terms of brain-processes of a certain sort, the identity statement, 'The experience of pain at t = certain brain-processes at t', is either *necessarily* true or is not the kind of contingent statement (about the relation of experiences and brain-processes) with which we are concerned. If the statement is to be both contingent and of the relevant kind, the analysans of 'the (apparent) perception of a yellow lemon at t' must be both logically independent of all ϕ-descriptions of brain-parts, and must in some way describe experiences *as such*. These requirements, I would suggest, compel us to introduce ψ-properties and

ψ-descriptions, for ψ-descriptions are both logically independent of ϕ-descriptions and characterize experiences *as such*.

Smart might reply that I am overlooking a distinction between non-connotative referring terms or pure referring terms, and connotative referring terms or identifying descriptions. He might argue that we *can* formulate an appropriate contingent identity statement: 'Smith = the first man to climb Mt. Everest', or 'e = certain brain-processes at t', in which one term is a pure referring-expression ('Smith', 'e'), the other an identifying description ('the first man to climb Mt. Everest', 'certain brain-processes at t'). There are no logical connections between one term and the other and we may therefore coherently articulate the contingent identity-statement with which we are concerned.

The reply, though tempting, will not do. The implicit assumption that pure referring terms can function in complete isolation from any identifying description of their referent(s) is entirely misguided. It is certainly true that we may use pure (or very nearly pure) referring terms to pick out individuals—referring terms which are not logically connected in any straightforward sense with the relevant singular descriptions. But they can be used in this way only with a *backing* of singular descriptions, that is, only if we are prepared to pick out the individual to which the pure referring term putatively refers, by means of a singular description. I cannot use 'Fido' of Fido unless I can if necessary provide a descriptive backing for 'Fido', unless I can pick out Fido as that dog over there or as the winner of Cruft's etc. So, although the necessity or contingency of identity-statements in which pure referring terms occur is not a simple function of the kinds of description employed in them, it *is* a function of (*inter alia*) the description or descriptions which are taken to be the 'backing' for the pure referring term. Consider certain examples. Let us suppose that 'X' refers to a triangular figure drawn on a sheet of paper. It makes no sense to claim that 'X = that three-sided figure' is contingent or necessary until we know what identifying descriptions might be used to back up the use of 'X'. If the description is understood to be 'that three-sided figure', the identity-statement in question will be necessarily true; if it is understood to be 'John's latest drawing', the statement will be contingent. Similarly, if 'X' referred to the number 2, it would be odd in the extreme to claim, without

qualification, that 'X = the only even prime number' is contingent
—odd, not because of any temptation to claim that the statement
is necessary but rather because we require more information about
X than is conveyed by the use of 'X', to decide the exact logical
form of the identity-statement.

So, to summarize the objection again: I have argued that the
contingency or necessity of an identity-statement is a function of
the kinds of description we employ in it; I have pointed out that
the only non-circular description of experiences that Smart allows
is a description of them as brain-parts having certain ϕ-properties.
He is therefore unable, within the linguistic resources he allows
himself, to formulate the appropriate contingent identity-statements, and is therefore committed to rejecting the Contingency
Thesis. As I have pointed out already, this should be regarded
as a distinctly embarrassing consequence of his position, since
he bases his philosophical thesis on a certain set of scientific
claims about the relation of experiences and brain-processes. But
if the relation in question is that of logical necessity, it cannot be
the topic of any scientific investigation at all. It is worse than
pointless to engage in the experimental investigation of an *analytic*
relation between two individuals. The most satisfying solution of
Smart's difficulties, as I have already suggested, is to admit that
experiences have introspectible phenomenal content, that certain
brain-parts have ψ-properties. For, since there are no logical
relations holding between ϕ- and ψ-properties, he can characterize
experiences in terms of ψ-properties and so formulate the
appropriate contingent identity-statements.

It is important to stress 'appropriate'. There are clearly many
inappropriate contingent identity-statements in this area—for
example, 'Brain-part P_1, discoloured at t_1 = Brain-part P_2 at t_2'
or 'Brain-part P_3, decomposing at t_3 = Brain-part P_4, prodded
at t_4' . . . etc. These statements, each term of which refers to the
ϕ-properties of brain-parts, are not appropriate to the Identity
Theorist's enterprise. They are inappropriate because they
involve no reference whatever to experiences *as such*; and a crucial
feature of the Identity Theory is the claim that there is a contingent
identity between experiences of a certain kind and brain-processes
of a certain kind. It is crucial in so far as the theory is to be an
interesting hypothesis competing with other hypotheses (e.g. that
experiences are identical with liver-processes or with magnetic

fields or with vibrations of the ether). So the Identity Theorist cannot merely be content to produce contingent identity-statements, each term of which characterizes brain-parts *in some way or other;* at least one of the terms must explicitly acknowledge the occurrence of an *experience* (identical with a certain brain-state or process). It is interesting to note, incidentally, that Smart seems to slide into discussing *inappropriate* contingent identity-statements. For example, on pages 8–9 of *Philosophy and Scientific Realism,* he says: '. . . I shall be concerned to argue for the plausibility of the view that the human brain is no more than a physical mechanism, that no vitalistic or purely psychical entities or laws are needed to account for its operations.' This, no doubt, is an interesting view but is hardly the Identity Theory as we know it. What has to be proved is not the identity of the *brain*, but the identity of the *mind*, with a physical mechanism.

5. *Phenomenal Properties and Contingency* (2)

The Materialist—i.e. the Identity Theorist who wishes to deny that there are any introspectible phenomenal properties—might argue that I have overlooked one very important suggestion. He will argue that he might circumvent the difficulties we have examined by characterizing experiences in the way suggested by Armstrong,[10] namely as those states of the brain which are apt to produce certain kinds of behaviour. And certainly it would be very foolish to overlook Armstrong's very important contribution to the discussion. Not merely does he present us (for the first time) with detailed analyses of a large number of mental states (some of which we shall examine in Part IV). More importantly, he is very much aware of the implications of the Contingency Thesis:

. . . if 'The mind is the brain' is a contingent statement, then it follows that it must be possible to give logically independent explanations (or, alternatively, 'ostensive definitions') of the meaning of the two words 'mind' and 'brain' . . . The problem is posed by the word 'mind'. What verbal explanation or 'ostensive definition' can we give of the meaning of this word without implying a departure from a physicalist view of the world? This seems to be the great problem, or, at any rate, one great problem, faced by a Central-state theory.[11]

[10] D. M. Armstrong, *A Materialist Theory of the Mind, passim.*
[11] Ibid., pp. 77–8.

And his suggested solution of the problem is to characterize mental states in terms of their causal properties or causal 'aptitudes': 'The concept of a mental state is primarily the concept of *a state of the person apt for bringing about a certain sort of behaviour.* Sacrificing all accuracy for brevity we can say that, although mind is not behaviour, it is the *cause* of behaviour.'[12] To refer to experiences in that way is to make no reference whatever to phenomenal content, to the phenomenal properties of the brain and nervous system.

Consider then our original example: 'My (apparently) perceiving a yellow lemon at t = certain brain-processes at t.' The right-hand side of the identity-statement will be expanded into a statement about a brain-part and its ϕ-properties, the left-hand side into a statement about certain causal transactions, or potential causal transactions, between a physical state and other physical states. My (apparently) perceiving a yellow lemon at t is a state of my brain and nervous system apt to make me clutch at the table in front of me, or reach for sugar and eggs so that I may make a lemon pie filling, and so on. Similarly, a sensation of pain is a state of the brain and nervous system which is apt to make me apply a dressing to the afflicted part, to make me groan, grimace, etc.; the perception of a brick wall is a state apt to make me drive around it; and so on.

On closer examination we see that the suggestion is promising only because of the convenient vagueness of experiences like 'apt for' and 'certain kinds of behaviour'. It is by no means as clear as Armstrong appears to think, that we could ever concisely and comprehensively describe the entire range of behaviour which any given experience is apt to provoke. Unless he can offer such a concise and comprehensive description he cannot ever guarantee that he has uniquely identified the experience which he wishes to identify. If two qualitatively dissimilar experiences (e.g. a headache and a thought about a difficult philosophical problem) are both apt for the production of precisely the same kind of behaviour (e.g. frowning, clutching one's forehead, not paying attention, etc.), Armstrong will be unable to distinguish them satisfactorily in terms of their causal properties.

Even if we overlook this initial difficulty, the difficulties which afflicted Smart's position prove equally devastating to Armstrong's.

[12] Ibid., p. 82.

For example there is the problem of expanding the phrase 'state which is apt . . .' We must beware of expanding it into a statement of the form 'brain-state of *such-and-such* a kind which is apt . . .', for if the expansion is too comprehensive, the two sides of the relevant identity-statement will be virtually the same and it will be necessary not contingent. Moreover, not all states which are apt to produce certain behaviour are states of *consciousness*, experiences. That is, it is by no means clear that Armstrong can ensure that his contingent identity-statements are 'appropriate', that they include reference, explicitly or implicitly, to a person's awareness of his experiences *as such*.

And here is the rub. For a person is not aware of all of his experiences *as* states apt to produce certain behaviour. Indeed one could even say that a person is very rarely aware of experiences as apt to produce anything whatever. Certainly a reflective person will notice that a severe pain is apt to make him feel faint or clutch his brow in agony, or that his remembering some sin of omission is apt to make him blush or groan or rush to the telephone. But it is certainly not true that we are generally aware of our experiences as having certain causal properties. Anyone who thinks that we are might try to articulate the causal properties of the following experiences: hearing a solitary middle C, the kinaesthetic sensations associated with sitting down, perceiving the left foot, perceiving the right foot, touching an ordinary polished table. The point of choosing trivial experiences is that they are trivial, but experiences none the less. Without a great deal of imagination it is difficult to see what causal 'aptitudes' they might have, and so, *a fortiori*, it is implausible to suggest that we are aware of them *as having* certain causal 'aptitudes'. So to characterize them in that way is not to characterize them as experiences, and Armstrong is trapped in Smart's dilemma. He must refer to experiences as such or not as such. If he refers to them *as* experiences he is compelled to admit a phenomenal element in experience; if he fails to refer to them *as* experiences then the identity-statements he formulates in the course of the argument are *either* appropriate but necessary *or* contingent but inappropriate. In the first case he is committed to rejecting the Contingency Thesis and in the second he is not talking to the point.

The Materialist might make a final attempt to evade all the

difficulties I have described, by characterizing experiences in very general terms as 'those things which were referred to as "pains" or as "thoughts" ' or as 'those things which some philosophers believe to have introspectible phenomenal content'. That is, he abandons the search for extensional properties of experiences and resorts to characterizing them in terms of their intensional properties. In doing so he certainly extricates himself from his immediate difficulties, for a property such as 'referred to as a pain' or 'believed to have phenomenal content' is logically independent of the physical properties of brain-parts, and so (when translated into our rather cumbersome language of 'ψ-ish-ness') allows us to formulate identity-statements which are both appropriate and contingent.

But in doing so he undermines the whole physicalist enterprise —to identify experiences with brain-processes. It will be remembered that the first stage of that enterprise is the Correspondence Hypothesis, the general scientific claim that whenever an experience of a certain (specifiable) kind occurs a physical state of a certain (specifiable) kind occurs. We begin then with a material equivalence between statements of the form 'A ψ-ish experience occurs at t' and statements of the form 'A ϕ-ish physical state occurs at t.' Now if the Materialist is prepared to substitute intensional predicates on 'ψ' at a later stage of his argument (in formulating contingent identity-statements), he must be prepared to substitute intensional predicates on 'ψ' at an early stage as well, the stage at which he formulates the Correspondence Hypothesis. But if we allow substitution of intensional predicates on 'ψ' in the Correspondence Hypothesis, it is a hypothesis which is straightforwardly false. For example suppose I occasionally misidentify Smith's thoughts about Napoleon as twinges of toothache. It will certainly be false that a certain event occurs in Smith's brain and nervous system if and only if a certain event occurs which is believed to be a twinge of toothache. To put the whole argument in a slightly different way: the Identity Theory is a complete non-starter unless statements of the form 'A ψ-ish experience occurs at t' are materially equivalent to statements of the form 'A ϕ-ish physical state occurs at t.' If we allow intensional predicates to be substituted on 'ψ' there is no such material equivalence. So again the Materialist is faced with a dilemma. He must admit the existence of (extensional)

ψ-properties, i.e. genuinely introspectible phenomenal properties, or he must abandon the Contingency Thesis.

Of course, he might argue, it is not incumbent upon us to maintain the Contingency Thesis at all costs. If it turns out that in attempting to formulate the contingent identity-statements which the thesis requires we find that we are committed to the existence of ψ-properties, we should simply abandon the Contingency Thesis. A description of our experiences wholly in terms of the non-introspectible responses of an organism to certain stimuli will be completely adequate for all our important purposes. Even if there *are* ψ-properties, the contingent identity of certain experiences with certain brain-states/processes would be sufficient to support an entirely non-phenomenal language. That is, he would argue, this basic but contingent feature of our world would allow us successfully to refer to certain experiences, even though we could never refer to them as experiences and could never describe the contingent feature in question. We should always, as it were, get the right answers but never be able to say why.

If the Materialist did say such things he would be horribly confused. To put it at its mildest, it is unclear how he can abandon the Contingency Thesis on the one hand and, on the other, still talk of 'the contingent identity of certain experiences with certain brain-states/processes . . . sufficient to support an entirely non-phenomenal language'. And as I have already pointed out, as soon as he abandons the Contingency Thesis he renders unintelligible the scientific inquiry upon which rests his whole philosophical position. One does not scientifically investigate logically necessary connections. But perhaps the most appropriate final observation on this excessively pragmatic proposal is provided by Smart, for, at the very least, he wishes to regard 'the physicist's picture of the world as an ontologically respectable one'.[13] Indeed 'As I propose to use the word "philosophy" it will stand primarily for an attempt to think clearly and comprehensively about . . . the nature of the universe. . . .'[14] It would seem a necessary condition of our thinking comprehensively, in a way which is 'ontologically respectable', that we give an account of all individuals and properties of individuals which are empirically discoverable in the kinds of situations to which the account is meant to be

---

[13] J. J. C. Smart, *Philosophy and Scientific Realism*, p. 47.
[14] Ibid., p. 1.

relevant. If there *are* ψ-properties an account of them must be given. I have already indicated at length why I think there are such properties and why the Identity Theorist is logically committed to admitting them into his picture of the world.

6. *Provisional Conclusions*

We leave this rather destructive first stage of the revisionary account with certain very positive results. We have distinguished the (scientific) Correspondence Hypothesis from the (philosophical) Identity Theory, and shown how Ockham helps us to move from the former to the latter; we have emphasized that an essential part of the Identity Theory is the Contingency Thesis, the claim that the identity of experiences with brain-states is contingent, not necessary; and we have shown that, if the Contingency Thesis is to be maintained, a materialist form of physicalism (i.e. a form of physicalism which leaves no room for introspectible phenomenal properties) is a non-starter, for it *either* generates identity-statements which are necessary and not contingent *or* generates identity-statements which are contingent but 'inappropriate'.

Earlier, after formulating the Identity Theory, I observed that there are two difficulties surrounding the notion of a phenomenal or ψ-property and the claim that ψ-properties are known directly by introspection, ϕ-properties by physiological investigation. We must show in what sense ψ-properties are *phenomenal* and in what sense they are *properties* of brain-parts. In battling with Smart and Armstrong we have provided part of a solution to the first difficulty. In the next chapter we shall provide the rest of the solution, together with a solution of the second. More generally we shall hope to justify my claim that ψ-properties can be accommodated within a physicalist account of persons without too much embarrassment.

5

THE REVISIONARY ACCOUNT

1. *The State of Play*

HAVING delivered a first blast of the trumpet against the monstrous regiment of physicalists—or rather the specifically materialist platoon of that regiment—we must pause to collect our thoughts before delivering a series of further blasts in Part IV. For there are two main tasks still to be attempted before the revisionary account is complete. First, although the argument with the materialist showed that a coherent version of the Identity Theory must make provision for phenomenal or ψ-properties, we have still not offered very explicit information about such properties; we have not wrestled with one or two difficulties which arise from trying to accommodate them within the theory. And second, we must formulate explicitly the account of persons to which the physicalist or revisionary metaphysician is committed. These two tasks will occupy us in the next two sections of the chapter.

However, before setting off it is perhaps helpful to summarize the version of physicalism which takes fully into account the criticisms of materialism. The general object of the exercise is to present an account which acknowledges in the most economical way the scientific Correspondence Hypothesis, and which is consistent with the Contingency Thesis. The simplest coherent account which appears to fulfil these requirements is essentially Feigl's position, 'raw-feel' physicalism.[1] Thus, experiences and brain-states are contingently identical in the sense that there are certain primary physical particulars—brain-parts, parts of a human brain and nervous system—which, besides possessing physical (or ϕ-)properties, also contingently possess certain phenomenal (or ψ-)properties at certain times. The account is physicalist because it involves insisting that there are only physical things in

---

[1] Cf. H. Feigl's *The 'Mental' and the 'Physical'*. In his postscript to the reprint of that paper, however, he appears to move towards materialism. I shall discuss the move in Section 4.

the world, that every individual is either a physical individual or reducible to a physical individual or a property of a physical individual (or, of course, a property of a property of a physical individual etc.).

We might note *en passant* one asymmetry between the ϕ- and ψ-properties of brain-parts, an asymmetry arising from the Contingency Thesis and from one of the scientific assumptions of the entire account. When the Identity Theorist was to make the move from *correspondence* to *identity* we asked, Under what description are the identical items to be identical? (or more crudely, What are the basic items?) Without the particular scientific assumptions we made, there was no better reason for making the physical than for making the phenomenal the descriptions under which experiences and brain-states are identical. Without those assumptions we could have constructed an Identity Theory in which the primary particulars were *phenomenal*, contingently possessing ('irreducible', 'emergent') physical properties.

However, having made those assumptions, having in effect refused to countenance a discontinuity between men and the rest of nature, our primary particulars are physical (the ψ-properties 'irreducible', 'emergent'). This being so, it would seem that there is an asymmetry between the ϕ- and ψ-properties of those primary particulars, parts of a brain and nervous system. For whereas it is necessary that they have *some* physical properties, it is contingent that they have any phenomenal properties at all. It is of course contingent that they have any determinate physical properties, just as it is contingent that they have any determinate phenomenal properties. But whereas the suggestion that they might have no phenomenal properties is logically quite in order, the suggestion that they might have no physical properties is self-contradictory.

2. *Phenomenal Properties: Difficulties and Obscurities*

Let us now concentrate our attention on certain residual difficulties and obscurities surrounding the notion of a phenomenal or ψ-property. There are really three questions to be answered here: first, is it significant, let alone true, to ascribe ψ-properties to brain-parts? Second, can one really admit the existence of ψ-properties and yet remain a physicalist? And third, are ψ-properties primitive and irreducible?

First, then, is it significant, let alone true, to ascribe ψ-properties to brain-parts? Before our scientific investigations provoked anyone to formulate the Identity Theory, it was clearly significant to ascribe a certain sort of ψ-properties to *people* (properties such as thinking, being in pain, feeling miserable, and so on). But it is not clear whether it makes any sort of sense at all to ascribe, say, being pain-ish or being thought-about-Napoleon-ish, to parts of a brain and nervous system. The revisionary metaphysician wishes to insist that it does make sense, that the unwieldy terms in which the new ψ-properties are expressed are at worst a tribute to his lack of ingenuity and at best a reminder that he cannot felicitously express his results without the aid of a completely new language.

Matters are none the less (he will say) fairly simple. Let us suppose that P is a certain brain-part. Clearly we can form a number of subject-predicate propositions with P as the subject, as follows: 'P is stimulated by certain electrical impulses from the optic nerve . . .', or 'P is located at p at t . . .', or 'P is slightly discoloured at t. . . .' We can isolate a number of predicates ('. . . is stimulated by certain electrical impulses from the optic nerve', '. . . is located at p at t', '. . . is slightly discoloured', and so on) and a number of corresponding properties (being stimulated by certain electrical impulses from the optic nerve, being at p at t, being slightly discoloured). Similarly, he will say, we might also isolate a number of 'phenomenal' predicates ('is pain-ish', 'is thought-about-Napoleon-ish', 'is depression-ish') and a number of corresponding 'phenomenal' properties (being pain-ish, being thought-about-Napoleon-ish, being depression-ish). And we can form propositions with P again as the subject, as follows: 'P is pain-ish', or 'P is thought-about-Napoleon-ish', or 'P is depression-ish.' These are as significant, as intelligible, as well formed, as the propositions consisting of P as subject and a ϕ-predicate as the predicate.

It might be objected, however, that if the enterprise is indeed so simple it should not be necessary to introduce such terribly long-winded and unwieldy ψ-predicates. But the reply to the objection is already available, if we cast our minds back to the remarks in the previous chapter on primary particulars (e.g. persons) and secondary (e.g. experiences, brain-states, brain-processes). Our ordinary non-physicalist language is concerned (*inter alia*) with people as the primary particulars and with their properties. The physicalist language, on the other hand, is concerned (*inter alia*) with brain-parts as the primary particulars and with their properties. It is of course true that, although the primary particulars of each language are different, some of their secondary particulars—notably experiences, brain-states, and brain-processes —will be the same. But *because* the primary particulars are different in each case (people in one case, brain-parts in the other) the elimination of reference to experiences in favour of reference to primary particulars and their properties will be quite different in each case. In short, the physicalist is forced to characterize ψ-properties in this rather long-winded way because he has no other way of characterizing them. He cannot use the P-predicates of our ordinary language to form propositions about the phenomenal properties of brain-parts, for P-properties are properties of people and ψ-properties are properties of brain-parts. To confuse them is to be guilty of a category-mistake or series of category-mistakes.

It is interesting to note, incidentally, that in constructing a new physicalist language from the ruins of the old, as it were, the revisionary metaphysician side-steps entirely a popular objection to the Identity Theory, an objection which has received much greater currency than it deserves. If we accept Leibniz's Law (as, I take it, we do) then it is at least a necessary condition of identity that the two things identified share all their extensional properties. Since brain-states do have spatial properties and experiences do not, we are invited to conclude that experiences cannot be identical with brain-states: '. . . it is not meaningful to assign spatial location to some kinds of mental phenomena, e.g., thoughts. Brain phenomena have spatial location. . . . Therefore, thoughts are not identical with any brain phenomena.'[2] If we are quite clear how to articulate the ψ-properties of brain-parts the objection misses the mark, for experiences and brain-states *do* share all their extensional properties, and are seen to do so if we describe them in the language of brain-parts and the properties of brain-parts. For example the spatial properties of that brain-part which is of a certain colour at a certain place at a certain time *are* the spatial properties of that which is thought-about-Napoleon-ish at a certain time.

[2] N. Malcolm, 'Scientific Materialism and the Identity Theory', p. 663.

Let us move on, then, to the second question about ψ-properties, namely, Can one really admit the existence of ψ-properties and yet remain a physicalist? At the moment I can see no very strong reason why one cannot, as long as one characterizes physicalism in the way I suggested earlier, as insisting that there are only physical things in the world, that every individual (in the logical sense of 'individual') is either a physical individual or reducible to a physical individual or a property of a physical individual (or, of course, a property of a property of a physical individual etc.). One does not insist that all the properties of the physical individuals in question must be *physical* properties, for some (namely ψ-properties), though certainly extensional properties, are not physical properties. It is only the materialist who wishes to insist that all the (extensional) properties of the primary physical particulars must be physical properties. The exact criterion for distinguishing physical or ϕ-properties from phenomenal or ψ-properties is unclear, but it seems to have something fundamentally to do with space, with the essential possession of spatial properties (or not, as the case may be). I do not offer the suggestion as a firm criterion but rather as a useful clue. It seems to be true that the possession of a ϕ-property *entails* the possession of spatial properties, the possession of a ψ-property does not (although, of course, our memory of the Contingency Thesis reminds us that it is *contingently* true that those things which have ψ-properties also have spatial properties).

I noted parenthetically in the previous chapter that one may wonder whether a dualism of properties represents any substantial advance on a dualism of things. Perhaps we might also begin to wonder whether a language in which the primary particulars are (*inter alia*) brain-parts represents any substantial advance on a language in which the primary particulars are (*inter alia*) persons. For the philosophically puzzling properties of persons seem to have turned up, only faintly disguised, in the form of tiresomely irreducible ψ-properties of brain-parts. The extent of the tiresomeness becomes evident if we turn to the third question of this section, Are ψ-properties primitive and irreducible? For it seems fairly clear that we must answer firmly, Yes. Our rather extended discussion of the Contingency Thesis in the previous chapter shows not merely that ψ-properties cannot be reduced to ϕ-properties but, more importantly, that a successful reduction makes nonsense of the Identity Theorist's claim that experiences and brain-states are contingently identical. Irretrievably connected with the problem of reducibility, however, is the problem of *emergence*, a problem we noted right at the beginning of the previous chapter. We have so far left open the question whether ψ-properties are properties only of a *complex* physical individual, or whether they can be explained in terms of the properties of the simplest parts of the organism in question. If they can be explained only as the properties of a *complex*, Smart and others will of course accuse the raw-feel physicalist, our revisionary metaphysician, of introducing 'emergent' properties and 'emergent' laws. And 'by an emergent law I mean one which relates to some complex entity, but which is in principle inexplicable in terms of the simple entities.'[3] It is perhaps gratuitous to point out that Smart considers the introduction of emergent properties as distinctly undesirable and that the reason for his antipathy towards them is fundamentally aesthetic. He wishes to introduce no more kinds of entity, no more laws, than are absolutely necessary. To introduce emergent properties and emergent laws is to complicate an otherwise formally simple theory.

Before we can reply to Smart's objection we must try to clarify two points. First, we must indicate what are to be taken as the relevant simple entities and what are to be taken as the relevant complex entities. This, curiously, is a matter on which physicalists have offered us very little information. They have failed to indicate for example whether the atomic or whether the sub-atomic are to be taken as the simplest things for the purposes of the theory, whether atoms or particles are to be the simple things of which complex physical things are composed. In his account of materialism Paul Feyerabend seems to regard the atomic as the simplest level of discourse: 'Materialism . . . assumes that the only entities existing in the world are atoms, aggregates of atoms and that the only properties and relations are the properties of, and relations between such aggregates.'[4] And if we remember that our general problem is one of reducibility, of emergence, it seems that he is right in settling for atoms rather than, say, particles, as the simple entities. For whereas it seems plausible

[3] Smart, *Philosophy and Scientific Realism*, p. 50.
[4] P. Feyerabend, 'Materialism and the Mind-Body Problem', p. 49.

to argue that the physical properties of a physical complex are reducible to (i.e. *deducible from*) the physical properties (including relational properties) of its atomic parts, it is implausible to suggest that the properties of the supra-atomic might be reducible to (i.e. *deducible from*) the properties (including relational properties) of the sub-atomic, of particles and groups of particles. Notoriously for example the causal regularities of the supra-atomic cannot be reduced to any causal regularities of the sub-atomic, for it is in principle impossible to articulate any causal laws governing the sub-atomic.

If that is indeed the case then our simple entities will be the atoms which make up certain molecular brain-parts, and the relevant complex entities will be molecular brain-parts or complexes of molecular brain-parts (large pieces of brain-tissue or large sections of the brain and nervous system). On scientific grounds it would seem reasonable to suppose that ψ-properties will be ascribed to *complexes* of this kind and not to *simples*. For in particular experiments designed to support the scientific Correspondence Hypothesis, we will no doubt be concerned to point out correlations between the physical state of a certain large section of a brain and nervous system and the occurrence of a certain experience, and this scientific claim will be reflected in the philosophical claim that a certain complex brain-part has both certain ϕ-properties and certain ψ-properties.

Second, we need to understand what Smart means when he talks of one thing's being explicable in terms of another, of a complex entity's being explicable or inexplicable in terms of simple entities. 'Explain' has all the disadvantages of 'reduce'. We frequently talk of *explaining* A in terms of B or *reducing* A to B, but it is not always clear in what sense 'explain' and 'reduce' are being used. In particular it is not clear whether I am implying that A and B are *logically* equivalent or not. If I say for example that the collision between car and wall explains a man's injuries, I am not implying that the collision and the injuries are logically equivalent, for causal connections are contingent. Or if I say that a physiological story explains the occurrence of my pains, visions, twitches, I do not imply, nor is it true, that physical and phenomenal terms are logically equivalent.

Smart has already used that sense of 'explain' at least once in insisting that a physicalist language offers explanations, but not

literal translations, of our ordinary experience-reports. But when
he refuses to countenance emergent properties and emergent
laws, when he insists that the complex must be *explicable* in
terms of the simple, he has to use a much stronger notion of
explanation; he must take 'A is explicable in terms of B' as
equivalent to 'The properties of A are *deducible* from those of B.'
To use the weaker notion of explanation, to imply that the relation
between complex and simple is contingent, is entirely self-
defeating for his purposes. To 'explain' (in the weaker sense) the
complex in terms of the simple would necessarily involve precisely
the sort of 'nomological dangler' that he abhors; it would involve
inductive generalizations of the form 'A-type properties (of
complexes) are always found in conjunction with B-type properties
(of simples).' He must refuse to admit into his philosophical
scheme any properties of complexes which cannot be straightforwardly *deduced* from the properties of simples, in the way in
which, for instance, the properties of a polygon can be *deduced*
from the properties of, and relations between, its constituent
parts.

Of the two kinds of property we have distinguished, ϕ-
properties and ψ-properties, no difficulties appear to arise with
ϕ-properties. It is reasonable to concede (I at any rate am prepared
to concede) that the ϕ-properties of complex brain-parts *can* be
deduced from the ϕ-properties of certain physical simples, in the
way that the properties of a polygon can be deduced from the
properties (including relational properties) of its parts. That is,
it seems reasonable to concede that the ϕ-properties of complex
brain-parts are not 'emergent'.

In complete contrast, it does not seem reasonable or even
intelligible to make the same claim about ψ-properties. If ψ-
properties of complexes are deducible at all, they are deducible
either from the ϕ-properties of simples or from the ψ-properties
of simples. The first alternative will not do, for it amounts to the
claim that the connection between experiences and brain-states is
necessary. In short, it amounts to the rejection of the Contingency
Thesis. But the second alternative is even less promising, for it is
not clear what it *means* to say that the ψ-properties of complex
brain-parts are deducible from the ψ-properties of simples.
Presumably the claim includes the claim that one could show
scientifically that certain simple brain-parts had certain primitive

ψ-properties from which the ψ-properties of the relevant complex could be deduced. But since we have already noted that ψ-properties are identified introspectively, it is overwhelmingly difficult to imagine what, if anything, could count as primitive ψ-properties of physical simples. For example it is overwhelmingly difficult to imagine what could count as the primitive elements of the ψ-property, being-thought-about-Napoleon-ish. Experiences are not items built from smaller pieces in the way that larger brain-parts are built from smaller. It is worse than futile, it is unintelligible, to suggest that we might identify the primitive elements of an experience (the primitive ψ-properties of physical simples) and thereby deduce the content of the complete experience (the ψ-property of the complex brain-part).

In short, it seems that, if we are to talk of ψ-properties at all, we must accept that they are 'emergent' properties, properties of complexes which cannot be deduced from the properties of the simples which constitute the complex. But while this result is no cause for rejoicing, it is no cause for embarrassment either. Obviously one of the following theses must be rejected:

1. there are 'emergent' properties of physical complexes;

2. the conceptual apparatus of present-day physics (which leaves no room for 'emergent' properties and 'emergent' laws) is entirely comprehensive and satisfactory.

I see no very good reason for maintaining the second thesis at the cost of the first. The scientist will have to reconcile himself to including in his system somewhat heterogeneous properties and laws—on the one hand, laws connecting the properties of simples with the deducible (i.e. ϕ-)properties of complexes, and on the other, laws concerning the non-deducible 'emergent' (i.e. ψ-)properties of complexes. If he is to give a comprehensive account of physical phenomena, he has no alternative; and in this situation entities will not have been multiplied beyond necessity. Smart has said: 'By "materialism" I mean the theory that there is nothing in the world over and above those entities which are postulated by physics (or, of course, those entities which will be postulated by future and more adequate physical theories).'[5] But it is possible that we might be compelled to postulate laws of emergence as part of our future and more adequate physical theories, in order to give a comprehensive account of the ψ-properties of physical organisms.

[5] J. J. C. Smart, 'Materialism', p. 651.

Indeed the problem of emergence turns out to be yet another variation on a theme with which I have dealt at length—the need to postulate ψ-properties in order to articulate the Correspondence Hypothesis and the Contingency Thesis. If they are to be articulated, if the correlation between experiences and brain-states is to be contingent, we must have psycho-physical laws correlating two logically independent kinds of event or two logically independent kinds of property, φ- and ψ-properties. That is, from the argument in the previous chapter against materialism, it follows that ψ-properties cannot be reduced to the φ-properties of simples. If we cannot make sense of the notion of ψ-properties of simples, it follows in turn that ψ-properties are emergent, properties of complexes which cannot be reduced to the properties of simples.

One final thought on emergent properties. In the course of this book, at least three words have complicated the discussion at odd times because of their systematic ambiguity. One was 'mind', another was 'reduce', a third was 'explain'. We have now encountered a fourth, 'physical', which has been used in this and the previous chapter in two quite different senses. The first sense of 'physical' occurs when we talk of 'physical' or φ-properties, properties which are quite different from 'phenomenal' or ψ-properties. The second sense of 'physical' occurs when we talk of physics: 'physical' things and properties are those in which the physicist is interested. And if our discussion of emergent properties is correct, some 'physical' properties in this *second* sense of 'physical' will be 'phenomenal' or ψ-properties. Having pointed out the ambiguity, there is perhaps very little more to be said—although one might doubt whether the distinction between the 'physical' and the 'non-physical' in the *second* sense of 'physical' really adds up to very much. After all, if physics is physicalist in *that* sense of 'physical', it seems to be an extraordinarily comprehensive subject.

I have no wish to pursue the doubt, except in so far as it bears on a previous point: if physicists *are* to leave room for emergent properties and emergent laws, and if physics is indeed to be physicalist in an interesting sense, my original definitions of scientific physicalism and philosophical physicalism (at the beginning of Chapter 4) may need qualification. *Scientific* physicalism, I said, is the claim that all organic phenomena can be scientifically explained and predicted in terms of those concepts and laws which serve to explain and predict inorganic phenomena, namely the concepts and laws of physics; and *philosophical* physicalism is the claim that any coherent statement about an organic individual can be reduced to a statement or set of statements about inorganic individuals. If scientific physicalism is to remain true in the face of emergent properties and if philosophical physicalism is to be even remotely plausible, we must explain that organic things for the physicist are only complexes of inorganic things. It may be true that some of the properties of complex inorganic things are not reducible to the properties of simple inorganic things. But even allowing room for emergent properties, physics is still physicalist in the sense that the basic individuals of physics are spatio-temporal inorganic things ('physical' things in the first sense).

3. *The Physicalist Concept of a Person*

Since the general purpose of the inquiry is to compare two accounts of the concept of a person, the previous chapter and the first two sections of this chapter have really amounted to a set of preliminary investigations—investigations which must be made before we can state the full account of persons to which the revisionary metaphysician is committed. He has moved from the Correspondence Hypothesis (which correlates experiences and brain-states) to the Identity Theory (which identifies them). By insisting that the identity of experiences and brain-states is contingent he is committed to being a 'raw-feel' physicalist rather than a materialist, to leaving room for an account of the phenomenal content of experience.

It requires very little imagination to formulate the full account of persons to which he is committed. If he is to acknowledge the demand for economy and scientific realism, it will in general consist in the claim that all statements about persons will be reducible to statements about complex physical organisms. And were it not for the existence of 'emergent' ψ-properties, these statements in turn would be reducible to statements about simple physical individuals and their properties. It is no exaggeration to say that he is in effect inviting us to drop the word 'person' from our language and to introduce another word, typographically identical, but with a wholly different meaning. In the former sense of 'person' the proposition 'persons are merely physical organisms' is synthetic and false; in the new physicalist sense of 'person' the proposition 'persons are merely physical organisms' is analytically true.

It will be remembered that we summarized the descriptive account of persons in six theses, as follows:

1. the reference in a particular context of a personal pronoun (or the meaning of a personal possessive adjective) is the same, whether coupled with an M- or P-predicate;

2. both M- and P-predicates can be significantly (truly or falsely) coupled with terms referring to people;

3. M- and P-expressions (and, *a fortiori*, M- and P-predicates) are of different categories;

4. the concept of a person is logically primitive, prior both to that of a mind, and to that of a human body;

5. mental identity is sufficient but not necessary for personal identity; bodily identity is both defeasibly sufficient and defeasibly necessary for personal identity;

6. the connection between a particular person and a particular set of experiences, *qua* experiences of a certain type or types, is contingent; the connection between a particular person and a particular set of experiences, *qua* particular experiences, is necessary.

We shall perhaps appreciate the exact scope of the revision entailed by the physicalist's proposals, if we examine their impact on each of these six theses.

Superficially it would seem that if we read 'ϕ- and ψ-expressions' for 'M- and P-expressions' throughout, there will be very little disagreement between descriptivist and physicalist. Certainly it would seem that the physicalist would accept the first three theses without demur—the univocality thesis, the claim that M- and P-properties (or ϕ- and ψ-properties) can be significantly ascribed to people, and the claim that M- and P-expressions (or ϕ- and ψ-expressions) are of different categories. But the appearance of agreement is thoroughly misleading, for the physicalist can only accept the first three theses by interpreting them in a rather peculiar, rather strained, way, by qualifying them out of all recognition.

The source of the peculiarity, the strain, the qualifications, is his account of ϕ- and ψ-properties. Let us divide the qualifications into two. First, it will not do, without further comment, to suppose that references to M- and P-predicates or M- and P-properties can be translated straightforwardly into references to ϕ- and ψ-predicates or ϕ- and ψ-properties. For M- and P-properties are ascribed to people (as understood by the descriptivist), ϕ- and ψ-properties to brain-parts. Second, people as understood by the descriptivist are not the same as people as understood by the physicalist. For the descriptivist people are primary or basic particulars, whereas for the physicalist they are not: they are complex physical organisms composed of the physical simples (including simple brain-parts) which are his basic or primary particulars.

Thus, our physicalist analyses of statements like 'John is tall', 'Jill is fat', 'James is thinking', 'Joan is depressed', will turn out to be rather complicated in some cases. The analyses of statements containing M-predicates will be (comparatively) less complicated, for predicates such as 'is tall', 'is fat', 'is solid', 'is at p at t', and so on, will survive and will continue to be coupled with names and personal pronouns. The names and pronouns of course will be taken as referring to complex physical organisms. But the analyses of statements containing P-predicates will be (comparatively) very complicated, for predicates such as 'is thinking', 'is depressed', 'is planning a holiday', and so on, will not survive at all (at any rate will not retain anything like their original meaning). All statements in which P-predicates were coupled with names and personal pronouns, for example, will be replaced by (or interpreted as) statements in which ψ-predicates are coupled with expressions referring to (complex) brain-parts. When I say 'Jill is thinking about a holiday' I am to be interpreted as saying something of the form, 'A certain brain-part P which is part of that physical organism over there (let us call it "Jill") is thought-about-a-holiday-ish.' If the descriptivist and the physicalist both talk of P-expressions, we should not suppose that they are both talking of the same kinds of expression.

So we see after all that there is a large area of disagreement between the descriptivist and the physicalist over the first three theses of the descriptive account, a disagreement which tends to be disguised unless one goes to the trouble of spelling out the physicalist interpretation of each thesis. What then of theses 4, 5, and 6 (the claim that the concept of a person is primitive, the statement of the general criteria of personal identity, and the statement of the general criteria of identity of experiences)? It seems that a physicalist must deny them all, that he must make the following claims:

4P. the concept of a person is not logically primitive, but is logically equivalent to that of a certain (i.e. human) physical organism;

5P. bodily identity is both necessary and sufficient for personal identity;

6P. the connection between a particular person and a particular set of experiences, *qua* experiences of a certain type or types, is contingent; and the connection between a particular person (= body) and a particular set of experiences, *qua* particular experiences, is contingent, not necessary.

Since 6P is a consequence of the Contingency Thesis, we may concentrate on 4P and 5P. If people are essentially complex physical organisms, it would seem that the concept of a person collapses without remainder into the concept of a human body, and that problems about personal identity are entirely exhausted by problems about bodily identity.

However, it may be that appearances are again deceptive, that matters are really much more complicated, that the Contingency Thesis may yet again have important consequences which it is all too easy to overlook. For if ψ-properties of brain-parts are to act as some kind of substitute for the P-properties of people, it may be that the physicalist cannot maintain that personal and bodily identity are logically equivalent. The difficulty is of considerable interest and importance in the inquiry but I prefer to postpone its full consideration until certain other problems have been considered. This arrangement of the argument will, I hope, prove to be convenient.

4. *Back to Materialism?*

The revisionary account is now essentially complete. It is in outline the 'raw-feel' physicalism which Feigl set out in the first version of *The 'Mental' and the 'Physical'*. It leaves room for emergent irreducible phenomenal properties, and is in that sense a rather diluted form of physicalism. However, since one should be aware of different versions, greater refinements, of physicalism, because many physicalists would not be satisfied with a 'diluted' account, it is only fair to examine the recent changes in Feigl's position. When discussing the problem of emergent properties I observed that some might doubt (although I did not) whether an account which leaves room for emergent properties really deserves the title 'physicalism' at all. The contrast between the physical and the non-physical might seem to collapse if physics is to take account of emergent 'phenomenal' properties, to take account of everything.

Feigl seems to have been so much impressed by doubts of that kind that he has proposed a much more thoroughgoing physicalism in which phenomenal properties are discarded altogether. In the Postscript to the reprint of *The 'Mental' and the 'Physical'* he offers a few suggestions as to how this might be done. In doing so he apparently rejects 'raw-feel' physicalism in favour of materialism. The entire enterprise, the formulation of a 'thoroughgoing physicalism', as I called it, really has three stages. First, attention is drawn to an extensional equivalence between statements reporting certain mental events and statements reporting certain physical events—that is, we formulate the Correspondence Hypothesis. Second, the mental events are identified with the physical events. These two stages of the argument have occupied most of our attention in Part III. But the third, and by far the most radical, stage is the construction of an entirely physicalist language. There are various ways of describing the enterprise. One is to say that physicalist analyses of all mental states are offered; another is to say that all expressions referring to mental states as such are discarded in favour of (extensionally equivalent) expressions referring to physical states; yet another is to say that our ontological scheme is cut down to size by discarding all ψ-properties in favour of (coextensive) ϕ-properties. All the ψ-properties we have been so careful to preserve in the arguments of Part III will be replaced by what Feigl calls physical 'successor-concepts':

> . . . just as the common sense (direct-realist) concepts of surface colour, tone quality, flower fragrance, heat intensity, tangible hardness, etc. are supplanted by their 'successor' concepts (a felicitous term used by W. Sellars) in physical theory, such as frequency of electromagnetic waves, frequency, etc. of acoustical waves, chemical structure of 'aromatic' compounds, molecular motion, atomic structure (of, for example, the diamond), etc.—so the phenomenal predicates used in

the description of after-images, sensations, feelings, emotions, moods, etc., are to be replaced by the (as yet only sketchily known) neurophysiological and ultimately micro-physical characterizations.[6]

'Emergent' properties will therefore be no more:

Inasmuch as a good and complete physicalistic . . . account of the world will contain 'successor' concepts to all phenomenal concepts, there will indeed be no 'nomological danglers' in such an account. Nothing important is omitted in such a description; but, of course, what counts as 'important' are the spatio-temporal-causal features that are essential for the world's description, explanation, prediction, and retrodiction.[7]

In short, if we embark on the third stage, 'raw-feel' physicalism seems to collapse into materialism, albeit a very sophisticated materialism.

Feigl only offers a sketch of the thoroughgoing physicalism with which he now finds himself in sympathy, and offers no specific analyses of particular mental states. For examples of such analyses we must turn (and shall frequently turn) to a materialist whom we have already encountered—Armstrong.[8] He investigates a wide range of topics (the will, knowledge, perception, the secondary qualities, mental images, bodily sensations, introspection, belief, and thinking) in an effort to show in detail that a radical physicalist programme can be successfully carried out.

Purists will no doubt object that if 'raw-feel' physicalism collapses into materialism, it is open to all the devastating objections we examined in Chapter 4, that it is therefore not worth our attention, and that we may now bring the whole inquiry to an abrupt end. However, I propose to ignore them for at least two reasons. First, although it is fruitful to confront the physicalist at every turn with the implications of the Contingency Thesis, the objection does tend to lose its interest if worked too hard. Although it was valuable in pointing out the incoherence of materialism (and would continue to do so, if we wished to use it yet again), we should not forget that there may be other interesting objections to physicalism still to be explored. Second, as we shall see in the course of Part IV, the difficulties which eventually undermine physicalism do not arise principally at its third stage (the final construction of a thoroughgoing physicalist language)

---

[6] Op. cit., pp. 141–2.   [7] Ibid., p. 144.
[8] Cf. Armstrong's *Materialist Theory of the Mind, passim.*

but are rather more closely concerned with the first, at which is established an extensional equivalence between statements reporting certain mental events and statements reporting certain physical events. We shall examine the notion of analysis which inspires physicalist 'analyses' of mental states, but this will in turn be more of a problem about extensional equivalence (about the first stage) than a problem about analysis (about the third stage).

5. Retrospect

Finally let us look back briefly at the revisionary account of Part III. I began by distinguishing scientific from philosophical physicalism and pointed out that it is possible to accept the former and reject the latter. I then examined two varieties of philosophical physicalism—materialism, which deliberately leaves no room for the (so-called) phenomenal content of experience, and 'raw-feel' physicalism, which does. I showed how the Contingency Thesis commits one to rejecting materialism and accepting 'raw-feel' physicalism, which thus became the nucleus of the revisionary account of persons, the account which is to confront the descriptive account outlined in Part II.

In the course of the argument I have expressed a number of doubts about the general enterprise or about particular features of it. For example I wondered whether a dualism of properties represented any important advance on a dualism of substances or things, and whether a language whose primary particulars are brain-parts is any better than a language whose primary particulars are people. For the philosophically puzzling P-properties of people seem only faintly disguised as equally puzzling ψ-properties of brain-parts. There was also doubt as to whether the physicalist could sustain the claim that personal identity and bodily identity are equivalent, for the Contingency Thesis may once again prove to have very important consequences. And finally we observed the changes in Feigl's original position, his apparent move towards materialism as a result of doubting whether a physicalism which leaves room for emergent properties is really physicalist. Perhaps over everything there is a general doubt, often expressed, about the importance of scientific work for philosophy. Some of the more important doubts require supporting argument which has so far not been forthcoming. It will, I hope, come forth in Part IV.

PART IV

EVALUATION

'The accusation of the Holy Office against Galileo stated that his thesis was philosophically absurd. A more crushing arraignment could not well be.'

(THOMAS MANN, *The Magic Mountain*, Ch. VI.)

6

TWO IMAGES OF MAN

1. *Complementary Images of Man*

WE are now at last in a position to compare the two accounts of persons presented in Part II and Part III. On the one hand we have the descriptive account, in which persons are regarded as basic or primary particulars; on the other we have the revisionary account, in which they are regarded merely as complexes of microscopic physical bits and pieces, and it is the microscopic physical bits and pieces (the most important of which are parts of brains and nervous systems) which are the basic or primary particulars. One offers us a language of people and their M- and P-properties; the other, a language of brain-parts and their ϕ- and ψ-properties (or, if we follow Feigl back into materialism, their 'successor' ϕ-properties). The questions originally posed in Chapter 1, and requiring an answer in this and the following chapters, were two: first, are the descriptive and revisionary accounts competitors? And second, if they are competitors, which account should we accept and why?

In assessing the physicalist's proposals we might first consider a rather interesting suggestion which yields a very clear decision on the issue. The suggestion is simply (and, perhaps, familiarly) that although the two accounts appear to be competitors they are in fact complementary. Wilfred Sellars for example, in his 'Philosophy and the Scientific Image of Man',[1] argues that a truly 'synoptic view' of the world can be obtained only by combining what he calls the 'manifest' and the 'scientific' images of man. Although he does not describe either image in detail, it is clear that his 'manifest' image of man is essentially that of the descriptivist and his 'scientific' image is that of the physicalist. The basic individuals of the manifest image are persons and material objects, those of the scientific image are the fundamental individuals of physical science (e.g. physical particles and complexes of physical particles). The two images are of course

[1] Ch. 1. of Sellars's *Science, Perception and Reality*.

logically independent of one another; prima facie they are therefore competitors and prima facie it is the scientific image which reflects the real structure of the world. However, he suggests, we should treat the two images as complementary. Indeed it is precisely *because* the categories of one image logically cannot be reconstructed in terms of the categories of the other, that

... to complete the scientific image we need to enrich it *not* with more ways of saying what is the case, but with the language of community and individual intentions, so that by construing the actions we intend to do and the circumstances in which we intend to do them in scientific terms, we *directly* relate the world as conceived by scientific theory to our purposes, and make it *our* world and no longer an alien appendage to the world in which we do our living ... to do so is ... to transcend the dualism of the manifest and scientific images of man in the world.[2]

Thus, although the scientific image reflects what really is, it does not offer a comprehensive picture of man. In particular it fails to give an account of intentions, of purposes, of reasons for acting. To account for our intentional and rational manipulation of 'the world as conceived by scientific theory' we must employ categories which are quite independent of the scientific image, namely the categories of the manifest image. Crudely, stereoscopic vision is achieved only by means of a certain conceptual or ontological versatility.

This would appear to be an important suggestion repaying serious consideration. However, there is undoubtedly a certain air of paradox in claiming that 'the conceptual framework of persons is not something that needs to be *reconciled with* the scientific image, but rather something to be *joined* to it.'[3] The justification for the manœuvre is presumably that we employ different conceptual frameworks, different 'images', for different purposes. We employ the scientific framework when we wish to describe or explain the real structure of the world; we employ the manifest framework when we wish to describe man's deliberate intervention in the events of that world, his conscious perception and intentional manipulation of the world around him. Indeed Sellars wants to insist that, strictly speaking, when we use certain categories of the manifest framework we are not *describing* at all: '... to recognize a featherless biped or dolphin or Martian as a

2 Ibid., p. 40.   3 Ibid.

person requires that one think thoughts of the form, "We (one) shall do (or abstain from doing) actions of kind A in circumstances of kind C". To think thoughts of this kind is not to *classify* or *explain*, but to *rehearse an intention*.'[4] And to rehearse an intention is presumably to do something (other than describe) or to take up a certain attitude.

But at this point the suggestion tends to become a trifle obscure. It is not clear what distinction Sellars is drawing between describing or explaining on the one hand, and rehearsing an intention on the other. Nor can one be very enthusiastic about his repeatedly claiming that the scientific image reflects the real structure of the world or tells us what really is. Most importantly he provides us with far too little argument to dispel the air of paradox surrounding the claim *both* that the two images have different ontological postulates, different categories, *and* that they are complementary. Our revisionary metaphysician will view the suggestion with contempt; he will argue that the conflict between the two accounts (or images) is so violent as to make any attempted reconciliation entirely disreputable. His own account, he will say, is perfectly adequate for all our purposes. Not merely is it internally consistent and scientifically respectable, it is, above all, comprehensive and requires no support from the manifest image, from the descriptive account.

In attempting either to defend or to attack Sellars's suggestion we defeat the original purpose of its introduction, namely to make a short cut, to offer a neat and rapid solution of our problems. The short cut is unattractive unless we go into the reasons for its adoption or rejection; but by the time those reasons had been elaborated it would not be a short cut at all. However, our efforts have not been entirely in vain, for we shall find that certain of Sellars's themes crop up again and again. We should regard this section as provoking certain doubts, as adding to (or perhaps fortifying) those doubts I expressed at the end of Chapter 5. That is, we should begin to ask what it means to say that one is describing the world as it really is; or whether there is or can be or must be a place for the language of intentions, reasons, purposes.

[4] Ibid., pp. 39–40.

2. *Conceptual Incompatibility*

So we must return to our starting-point, as if Sellars's suggestion had not been made at all. And the first question we must try to answer is, What exactly is meant by the claim that the descriptive account and the revisionary account are competitors? What sort of competition, what sort of conflict, do we have here? Perhaps the obvious initial suggestion is that two accounts are competitors if they have mutually contradictory ontological postulates (or, more strictly, sets of ontological postulates). For example an account which involves claiming that there is a God will 'compete' with any account which involves claiming that there is no God, for 'there is a God' and 'there is no God' are contradictories.

Unfortunately the suggestion does not seem in the least relevant to the matter in hand. Both the descriptivist and the physicalist make ontological claims of course ('there are persons, material objects, colours, sounds, experiences, . . . etc.'; 'there are particles, complexes of particles, simple brain-parts, complex brain-parts, . . . etc.'). But it is not clear that either is concerned to deny the ontological claims of the other. The descriptivist is not concerned to *deny* that there are particles, brain-parts, and so forth. Certainly he has failed to make very much provision for them, but the failure *is* a failure, not a *refusal* to do so. Similarly the physicalist will concede that in a very obvious, unscientific, unsophisticated way, there are persons and material objects; but for general scientific and philosophical reasons he is reluctant to complicate his account by referring to them as such, as macroscopic logically primitive things.

Indeed he would rapidly slide into incoherence if he attempted to deny that there are persons and material objects. Even if we remember that 'persons' has two senses, a descriptivist sense and a physicalist, he cannot succeed. Suppose he claims there are no persons in the *descriptivist* sense of 'persons'. Then at worst his claim is straightforwardly false, for there are obviously a large number of things answering the description (i.e. macroscopic material objects, possessing both M- and P-properties). At best he is expressing very elliptically his antipathy towards the descriptive account. But the ellipsis would not be a denial that there are persons. Suppose on the other hand that he claims there are no persons, in the *physicalist* sense of 'persons'. Then his claim is not

only false, for again there are obviously many things answering
the description (complex physical organisms of a particular size,
shape, composition), but also fails to make any relevant point
about the descriptive account. *Mutatis mutandis* similar disasters
overtake any descriptivist attempts to deny that there are particles,
brain-parts, and so forth.

So the first suggestion falls on very stony ground. Neither is
likely to want to deny the ontological claims of the other and
neither would succeed in doing so coherently in any case. Similar
problems arise with a second proposal. It might be suggested that,
although the ontological postulates of one account are not inconsistent with those of the other, certain of its general subject-
predicate propositions are inconsistent with certain subject-
predicate propositions of the other. For example let us suppose
we conjoin the following propositions, the first from the descriptive account, the second from the revisionary account:

1. 'It is not the case that people are merely complex physical
organisms.'

2. 'People are merely complex physical organisms.'

It looks as if we might be able to get some sort of argument going
here; and if we can, if 1 and 2 are mutually inconsistent, then we
can see clearly in what sense the accounts from which they come
are 'competitors', are mutually inconsistent.

Sadly 1 and 2 are entirely consistent with one another. We can
be misled into thinking otherwise only if we forget that there are
two quite different (*categorically* different) senses of 'person' or
'people'. 'People' in 1 does not mean the same as 'people' in 2;
each proposition has quite a different subject. 'People' in 1 has a
descriptivist sense ('those things to which M- and P-predicates
apply'), and 'people' in 2 has a physicalist sense ('complex
organisms of such-and-such a size, shape, and composition').
Indeed both 1 and 2 turn out to be analytically true. We could only
generate inconsistency if it were possible to offer an independent
description of people, a description common to both accounts.
But since the physicalist is attempting to replace the crucial concepts of the descriptive account by other concepts, no such
description is available.

Or is it? After all, both accounts appear to embrace the same set
of spatio-temporal concepts. We might try to describe people
simply in terms of their spatio-temporal properties in an attempt

to bridge the logical gap between the two accounts.[5] We might compare the following propositions:

1. 'That thing over there is not merely a complex physical organism.'

2. 'That thing over there is merely a complex physical organism.'

Undoubtedly, we now have the same subject and the same predicate in each case. Since the only difference between 1 and 2 is a negative particle, we appear to have a pair of mutually inconsistent propositions.

But once again the appearance is deceptive. For the word 'merely' changes the whole force of each proposition in such a way as to make them mutually consistent. It is quite clear what the descriptivist means when he says that that thing over there (i.e. some person) is not merely a physical organism: he wants to emphasize that it has certain P-properties as well as certain M-properties. People are physical organisms but not *merely* physical organisms. They have a number of properties (i.e. P-properties) which cannot be given a straightforward physical interpretation and which it is unintelligible, not merely false, to ascribe to material objects like tables and chairs.

The physicalist does not want to deny, nor can he deny, any of those things. He does not want to deny that people have P-properties, ascribable to them but not to other material objects. Nor, if the Contingency Thesis is to stand, does he want to insist that they can be given a straightforward physical interpretation. He wants rather to offer a very radical analysis of them. Proposition 2 cannot therefore be interpreted as denying that people think, feel, see colours, are depressed, etc. It can only be interpreted as insisting (elliptically) that thinking, feeling, seeing, etc. can all find a place in a physicalist language (the language for example of ψ-properties). But if 2 is insisting that some physicalist analogues of P-predicates can be articulated, and 1 is insisting that people have P-properties, 1 and 2 are perfectly consistent with each other.

If we cannot generate formal inconsistency between the ontological postulates of one account and those of the other, or between certain subject-predicate propositions of one and certain of the other, we have presumably no alternative but to offer a rather

[5] As Professor Antony Flew pointed out to me.

informal account of the supposed 'competition' or conflict between them. Perhaps the most illuminating, though philosophically crude, way of making the offer is to elaborate an analogy. Analogies are of course not arguments. But, remembering that Wittgenstein saw fit to express his later thoughts almost entirely in terms of an analogy (namely that of a game), perhaps we lesser mortals may be forgiven for resorting to one.

Suppose someone sends me a cake and I am trying to decide the best way to cut it up. I may cut it conventionally into equal parts by cutting across its diameters; or I may slice it vertically rather as I would slice a loaf; or I may slice it horizontally into flat discs; or I may cut it into tiny pieces so that I may see all the individual cherries, sultanas, etc., making up the cake; or I may, somewhat perversely, drop it on the floor so that I am left with entirely heterogeneous lumps of cake; and so on. However, although I can cut the cake in one of many ways, although I have many cutting-rules, and although I can visualize the cake cut up in various ways into pieces of different shapes and sizes, I shall only cut the cake *once*. I shall not *both* cut it into quarters *and* cut it into tiny morsels; I shall not *both* slice it vertically *and* slice it horizontally; and so on.

If we apply the analogy to the case in hand we see that our two accounts are two ways of cutting the world-cake. They are not mutually logically inconsistent, for they are only two quite different kinds of cutting-rule or two quite different ways of visualizing the world-cake cut up. But they are competitors in the sense that if I cut the world-cake into macroscopic quarters I shall not also cut it into microscopic morsels, for there is only one world-cake. The point of Sellars's suggestion, which we considered earlier, would be that I can if necessary cut different pieces of the cake in different ways. I may cut half of it into pieces large and small enough to eat; I may cut the rest into minute crumbs in preparation for a lesson on the physical structure of fruit-cake. For, as our revisionary confectioner will no doubt hasten to point out, the principle of the Unity of Science demands that all the properties of cakes in which domestic scientists are interested, are ultimately reducible to their *physical* properties.

It is rather difficult to treat our excursus into the philosophy (and physics) of domestic science with complete seriousness. But it does at least offer an informal answer to our first question.

That is, it does help to give some content to the notion of a conflict between two accounts of persons—but a conflict which is not straightforward logical incompatibility. Just as we have at least two different ways of cutting a cake, so we have two different ways of cutting the world-cake or the universe of discourse.

3. *Preliminary Objections to the Revisionary Account*

So much then for an informal answer to our first question. We now move on to the second, to consider the comparative merits of each account. The argument will fall into three parts. For the rest of this chapter we shall be concerned with a preliminary assessment of physicalism. I shall set out its supposed merits and consider certain rather feeble objections to it. In the next chapter we shall consider rather more devastating objections and finally in Chapter 8 we shall be in a position to examine general matters arising and to contemplate the comparative merits of the descriptive account.

The first thing to be done then is to consider why the physicalist thinks that his way of describing the world is better than the descriptivist's, why in particular he thinks that his account of persons is better than the descriptivist's. At the outset it is important to emphasize again that we are engaged in a philosophical rather than a scientific inquiry. We must assess the competing claims according to philosophical rather than scientific criteria. On a number of occasions I have emphasized the distinction between scientific physicalism (the thesis that for scientific purposes a comprehensive account of organic phenomena can be given in the physicalist terms used to describe and explain inorganic phenomena) and philosophical physicalism (the thesis that for philosophical purposes a comprehensive and accurate account of the world, in physicalist terms, can be given). We are engaged in assessing the revisionary account as a *philosophical* thesis, as a version of *philosophical* physicalism. The exact differences and connections between our scientific and our philosophical purposes will be pointed out when necessary in the course of the argument. At present we might say, in horribly general terms, that scientific purposes tend to be rather narrower than philosophical. The philosopher is concerned to give an analytical account of all kinds of individuals and properties of individuals which can coherently be postulated; the scientist on the other hand has the rather more restricted task of trying to predict any given event and explaining it as a function of certain other events. We should expect a scientific language to be comparatively stark and severe, very precise, and conceptually rather restricted.

When we remember the (philosophical) physicalist's obsession with science, it is easy to predict how he will support his claim that his account of persons is better than the descriptivist's. He has two main arguments. First, he will claim that the revisionary account is clear, coherent, and comprehensive. It is comprehensive in that it offers an account of all individuals which can significantly be distinguished, all individuals (and their properties) for which criteria of identification can be given. In contrast the descriptive account is not comprehensive. The descriptivist makes no attempt to classify, in a general way, the kinds of microscopic individuals which feature in scientific inquiry; he is interested only in giving a general account of the macroscopic individuals we normally encounter in sense-experience. It represents the ordinary beliefs of uncritical common sense, and uncritical common sense tends on the whole to be rather short-sighted. More importantly, perhaps, the beliefs of uncritical common sense are rather imprecise and at times even incoherent. When we put pressure on them (as we did in Chapter 3) we may find ourselves in considerable difficulty. There are large areas of the descriptive account (notably the notion of mental identity) which cannot be analysed very precisely. The physicalist claims to be offering simplicity and precision.

The second argument is that the revisionary account accords more with the facts revealed by scientific investigation (or the facts to be revealed by future scientific investigation). It is to be thought an advantage that our descriptions of the world reflect in some way its 'real' structure. In particular it is to be thought an advantage that the ways in which we describe persons reflect the results of physiological experiments. The descriptivist appears to be content with the set of concepts and categories which did service several centuries ago (or even earlier), despite spectacular advances in our scientific knowledge during the last century or so. Although, as we have seen, it is impossible to show that the descriptive account is inconsistent with scientific assumptions, it is clear that it does not reflect what we know about the microstructure of the macroscopic individuals (persons and material objects) with which it is primarily concerned.

Comprehensiveness, coherence, and scientific realism would seem to constitute an improvement according to some criteria. It is not clear that these are criteria of a philosophical kind; it is not clear that the revisionary account, *qua* comprehensive, consistent, and scientifically realistic, helps to solve or dissolve any philosophical problems which need solution or dissolution. Indeed many philosophers have made profound and important contributions to the philosophical study of persons despite their scientific handicaps. Aristotle could quite cheerfully continue to believe that the brain's function is to cool the blood; Descartes could without philosophical embarrassment argue that the circulation of the blood is due to its expansion and contraction in the heart, due in turn to changes in temperature. And conversely Kant's philosophical work would probably have been very much better had he made rather less frantic efforts to acknowledge the science of his day.

As we shall see in the following chapters, there are several difficulties afflicting the revisionary account. We shall see that there are strong grounds for doubting whether it is a coherent account, and for arguing that to talk of the 'real structure' of the world is to invite confusion. But at the moment I am concerned only to express certain doubts, to suggest that the advantages of the revisionary account are perhaps not philosophical advantages at all. I do not wish to articulate the doubts any more clearly at the moment, because we can only appreciate fully the point of raising them when the criticism of the revisionary account is complete. I shall return to them in the last chapter. To bring this chapter to an end I propose to consider a preliminary attack on the revisionary account, consisting of three rather feeble objections to the physicalist's proposals. It is convenient to clear them out of the way now so that we may get down to the more serious business in the next chapter.

The first objection takes us back to the scientific inspiration of physicalism. It seeks (quite reasonably) to regard physicalism as part of a much larger enterprise, namely the attempt to unify and systematize, within a deductive framework, the entire body of empirical discourse. If the demands for comprehensiveness and coherence are taken seriously, the physicalist will be committed to producing a physicalist language which works as rigorously as a formal calculus. All the predicates of the language will have precise criteria of application, the transformation rules of the language will be formulated rigorously, and so on. Körner has pointed out, for example, that 'The deductive unification of a schema of empirical differentiation by means of any of the existing logico-mathematical systems leads to the replacement of indefinite by definite individuals, of inexact by exact classes and relations, of relative by absolute continua.'[6] Our hypothetical objector claims that we are incapable of employing exact and only exact predicates, of identifying definite and only definite individuals, and so on; that indeed it is a necessary feature of empirical discourse as engaged in by human beings that we classify, describe, and differentiate individuals in a rather loose, inexact, occasionally unsystematic way. It is necessary both because of certain features of human beings and because of certain features of the things they talk about. On the one hand the complexity and rigour of the revised language we are envisaging would defeat us; we should be unable to use it with the precision it demands. And on the other hand there would always be individuals and properties of individuals which would not fit into the rigid framework of categories of the language; there would always be situations in which we should be unable to decide how exactly to describe what was going on. There would always for example be objects which were not quite red and not quite orange, or actions which were not quite deliberate and not quite involuntary or unconscious or unintentional, and so on. The revisionary language would not only demand an impossibly high standard of performance from its users, it would also demand an impossibly systematic ordering of Nature itself.

Although this objection deserves very little discussion, it is perhaps appropriate to note its weaknesses before passing on to the next. Its main point, I suppose, looks very much like a point I made at the end of Chapter 3 (and to which I shall return in Chapter 8). There I pointed out that the descriptive account really reflects certain limitations on our cognitive apparatus. We must identify rather macroscopic individuals (persons, material objects of a fairly chunky kind) because our sense-organs are comparatively clumsy (compared, that is, with many scientific

[6] S. Körner, *Experience and Theory*, p. 17.

instruments). But the two points are in fact rather different. The question, What individuals are to be distinguished? is rather different from the question, How precisely are they to be distinguished? The objection is concerned with the question of *precision*. And, as far as it goes, there is nothing to prevent the descriptivist from having *precise* criteria of identification for his rather *macroscopic* individuals.

Indeed (concentrating now on the main point of the objection) it is not clear that our ordinary empirical predicates are or must be inexact, that our basic individuals are or must be indefinite, and so on. On the contrary, in many cases it would appear that we do employ language in a precise and systematic way. J. L. Austin's 'A Plea for Excuses' is perhaps the most salutary attempt to show that many of us, including the redoubtable Finney of Regina *v.* Finney, constantly make very precise distinctions, use clearly defined predicates, in logically very complex circumstances. Finney was able to find his way through a very complex case while still distinguishing the intentional from the deliberate or the voluntary, or the unintentional from the inadvertent, the involuntary, the clumsy, the thoughtless, and so on.

The second objection seems a little more promising. It does not offer *a priori* forecasts about our ability to use a physicalist language, but criticizes it on the ground that it is misleading. It is argued that persons, however we conceive of them, are essentially those things which *experience*, which acquire knowledge of other things by means of sense-experience. One of the most striking and important features of the empiricist tradition, however unpalatable certain of its sceptical variations, is its emphasis on sense-impressions (ideas, sense-data), the most important raw materials of experience. A satisfactory account of persons can do justice to their importance only by giving prominence to them, and of course to other states of consciousness which are similar in some respects to sense-impressions (for example memory-experiences, images, etc.). The paralytic's eye-view gives no prominence whatever to states of consciousness.

The reply to this objection is very straightforward. We can if necessary give prominence in the revisionary account to certain epistemologically basic items by means, as it were, of a footnote. That is, we point out that in the complicated confrontation between human organism and environment the emergence of the ψ-

properties of parts of the organism is extremely important (and more than a trifle peculiar). Indeed we might do greater justice to that importance (and peculiarity) by describing the confrontation in terms of an information-flow model; the contact with the environment increases the organism's store of information.[7] Such a manœuvre is consistent both with the spirit and with the letter of physicalism. To demand greater concessions is to run the risk of lapsing into obscure mutterings about the 'felt quality of immediate experience', obscurity embarrassing for everyone.

4. *A Third Objection: Self-Consciousness and Conceivability*

The third objection, like the first, makes pessimistic forecasts about our ability to use a physicalist language, for equally obscure reasons. It is an objection standardly used in the free-will controversy against any thesis of determinism,[8] but is also relevant to our inquiry. It is argued that there is a crucial asymmetry between the first person and other cases, that one cannot coherently conceive of oneself merely as a physical organism. The spectator's view or, more strongly, the paralytic's eye-view, can be adopted only in observing the behaviour of other people. The fact of self-consciousness, the immediate awareness of oneself, precludes the possibility in one's own case of describing everything in terms of the properties of certain physical individuals, according to the principles of physics. If we are to take seriously Kant's argument in the Transcendental Deduction of the first *Critique*, we must make provision in our account of persons for self-consciousness. We must make provision for it because experience is possible only if I can ascribe my experiences to myself. For states of consciousness to enter consciousness at all, it must be possible for me to identify them in immediate self-consciousness as mine: 'It must be possible for the "I think" to accompany all my representations; for otherwise something would be represented in me which could not be thought at all, and that is equivalent to saying that the representation would be impossible, or at least would be nothing to me. . . .'[9] More generally, for experience to be possible at all,

---

[7] Cf. D. M. Mackay, 'Towards an Information-Flow Model of Human Behaviour'.
[8] Cf. J. E. Llewelyn, 'The Inconceivability of Pessimistic Determinism'.
[9] Kant, *Critique of Pure Reason*, B 131.

it must be such as to support a distinction between what is myself (or my states) and what is not:

> Now consciousness [of my existence] in time is necessarily bound up with consciousness of the [condition of the] possibility of this time-determination; and it is therefore necessarily bound up with the existence of things outside me, as the condition of the time-determination. In other words, the consciousness of my existence is at the same time an immediate consciousness of the existence of other things outside me.[10]

The weakness of physicalism (the objection goes on) is that it fails to acknowledge these crucial features of our experience, indeed that it cannot coherently acknowledge them. If experience is to be possible at all (or, in physicalist terms, if brain-parts are to have ψ-properties at all) I must be able to self-ascribe my states of consciousness, and so be able to distinguish between myself (and my states) and what is not. Physicalism cannot leave room for these conditions, for the simple reason that it leaves no room for the first person, for *myself*. There is no 'I', 'you', 'they', etc., only 'physical organism A', 'organism B, C, D, . . .' etc. The asymmetry between the first person singular and the second and third persons clearly disappears if there is no first person; no content at all is given to the notion of *my* consciousness of *myself*, of *my* distinguishing *myself* from what is not *myself*, if 'my' and 'myself' mean nothing more than 'physical organism A's', and 'physical organism A'. In short, if everything is referred to only in the third person (from the 'paralytic's eye-view') then there can be no way of articulating the Kantian necessary conditions of a possible experience. And this means that use of the physicalist language is self-defeating. To use it consistently to describe the world is to ensure that the necessary conditions of our experience of the world are not and cannot be fulfilled. We could not use the language to describe our experience because, if we were confined within such a language, there would be no experience.

We should be very careful in replying to the objection. We must do justice to the insights contained in it without being mesmerized by a rhapsody of selves and consciousnesses. The basic insights are clear: there is something logically absurd in the question, Are the experiences I am having really mine? There is also something

[10] Ibid, B 276.

logically absurd in talking of myself (and my experiences) unless I can distinguish myself (and them) from what is not. But it is not clear that the insights cannot be incorporated into physicalism. Indeed the fundamental asymmetry between the first person singular and other cases is already reflected in the physicalist's account of ψ-properties. Ψ-properties, he has said, are identified by introspection (the scanning of one brain-part by another), ϕ-properties by straightforward empirical observation. That is, the only organism able directly to identify organism A's ψ-properties will be organism A, and organisms B, C, D, etc. will have to be content to use other criteria (e.g. A's overt physical movements) to determine precisely the ψ-properties of A's brain-parts. The physicalist will be able to articulate the two Kantian insights very easily: on the one hand it will be logically absurd for A to ask, Are the ψ-properties of the brain-parts of organism A really the ψ-properties of the brain-parts of organism A? On the other there will be something logically absurd in A's referring to itself unless it can distinguish itself (and its ψ-ish brain-parts) from what is not.

Matters might become more complicated, I suppose, if the physicalism under attack is Smart's materialism or Feigl's later 'thoroughgoing' physicalism, in which ψ-properties are discarded in favour of their 'successor' ϕ-properties. Clearly if there are no ψ-properties, they cannot be identified by introspection and they cannot be used to articulate the Kantian conditions of experience. But it is still not clear that those conditions cannot be articulated at all. There is nothing to prevent the materialist, the 'thoroughgoing physicalist', from claiming that as a matter of (peculiar) fact each organism *does* have a peculiar access to some of the states of its brain and nervous system, an access denied to other organisms. The organism may not describe such states in sophisticated physical terms, for it may not have the physiological information available, but it is none the less directly aware of them. It will tend to fall back on very general classifications of such states, of the form 'What is going on in me is like what goes on in me when there is a pink elephant in front of me . . .' etc. The asymmetry between the first-person (or first-organism) case and other cases would be preserved, and the Kantian conditions could be expressed very easily as they were at the end of the previous paragraph, with ' "successor" ϕ-properties' in place of 'ψ-properties'. Of course, as we saw in Chapter 4, there are important difficulties in physicalist reductions of experience-reports to general classifications, but they are all connected with the need to express the Contingency Thesis. They have nothing to do with the need to express the Kantian conditions of experience. Those conditions can be expressed even within a very severe materialist language.

So the objection misses its mark. At its worst it appears to be a misunderstanding of the nature of self-consciousness; it appears to be a claim that self-consciousness is a consciousness of self, that is, an awareness of something other than a series of experiences. As Hume (or at least the Hume of Book I of the *Treatise*) seemed to suggest, and as Kant explicitly argued, the unity of self-consciousness, the principle of ordering of a series of experiences, is not yielded by a Cartesian soul or self in which all the experiences inhere. The unity of self-consciousness is a purely formal unity yielded by the subjects' awareness of experiences as his and by his awareness of himself as distinct from other things. The search for a self in self-consciousness is worse than a search for the Snark, and infinitely less entertaining. As soon as we understand what self-consciousness is not, we can understand how the physicalist can make provision for it in his account in the way I have suggested. For he can make sense of a person's immediate awareness of his experiences as his, and of his awareness of himself as distinct from other things.

At its best the objection collapses into a complaint that the words 'I', 'you', 'he', etc. will not feature in the physicalist language. But the complaint is obviously unjustified, if the peculiarities of our use of personal pronouns can be articulated in the physicalist language. If, as I have suggested, the physicalist *can* articulate the Kantian necessary conditions of experience, albeit in a physicalist language, there is no reason why 'I', 'you', 'he', etc. should not be part of that language. There is no reason for example why a complex physical organism should not describe himself in sentences beginning 'I am . . .', or why it should not describe others in sentences beginning 'you are . . .', 'he is . . .', etc.

So the third objection in its Kantian form fails to make any impression on physicalism. But we might find the objection restated in a slightly different form. The general claim is still that the revisionary account is peculiarly self-defeating, because inconceivable. However, whereas before we were concerned with one kind of inconceivability, we are here concerned with another. Before we were concerned with the need to express a man's immediate awareness of himself and his experiences; now we are concerned with the more general need to express one's own or other people's intentional behaviour. Indeed we are in a sense concerned with the need to express anything at all. The objection is simply that it is impossible intelligibly to state the revisionary account at all. Consider Malcolm's statement of the objection:

. . . there is a respect in which mechanism is not conceivable. This is a consequence of the fact that mechanism is incompatible with the existence of any intentional behaviour. The speech of human beings is, for the most part, intentional behaviour. In particular, stating, asserting, or saying that so-and-so is true requires the intentional uttering of some sentence. If mechanism is true, therefore, no one can state or assert anything. In a sense, no one can *say* anything. Specifically, no one can assert or state that mechanism is true. If anyone were to assert this, the occurrence of his intentional 'speech act' would imply that mechanism is false.[11]

That is, an utterance such as 'The revisionary account is true' would be self-defeating, rather in the way that it is self-defeating to say 'I speak no English whatever' or 'There is no truth; all truth is relative to one's social class or environment.' (It is unfortunately evident that many people, especially those of a Marxist persuasion, frequently make statements like the second without realizing their absurdity. If there is indeed no truth, it cannot be true that there is no truth.) It is self-defeating in that it rests on assumptions which it contradicts or makes use of categories which in some way it rules out of order. To utter the sentence 'The revisionary account is true' is to do something intentionally, with a certain purpose (namely to convince others), for a certain reason (presumably that the speaker thinks the revisionary account is true). Thus, to utter the sentence 'The revisionary account is true' is implicitly to acknowledge the categories of intentions, purposes, rational behaviour, while explicitly refusing to acknowledge them. One is not strictly contradicting oneself; 'The revisionary account is true' is not an instance of 'p & $\sim p$'. The revisionary account (logically) might be true even though one could never say so. It is inconceivable or unintelligible in the sense that, if it is true, then we do not have categories available to enable us to say so. And this is presumably a singularly embarrassing state of affairs.

There are two replies to the objection. One is simply to embrace it cheerfully, but to point out that we are not concerned with the conceivability of the revisionary account, but with its truth. We may be unable to articulate the paralytic's eye-view without involving ourselves in what might be labelled 'Malcolm's paradox', but it may still be the correct view. As the objector admits, there is no logical connection between the truth (or falsity) of a proposition and our ability (or inability) to conceive of its being true. Our failure to conceive the vastness of the heavens or the existence of fairies does not entail that the heavens are comparatively small or that fairies do not exist. It is perhaps regrettable that our philosophical research has shown that we shall never be able intelligibly to state the conclusions of the research, but we may console ourselves with the reflection that they are true.

The reply is very unattractive and I suggest that no physicalist could seriously entertain it. After all, if the categories of intentional, purposive, and rational behaviour are to be discarded, it will be absurd to talk of our having a reason for accepting his conclusions rather than the descriptivist's, of our choosing one account rather than the other as the right account. The physicalist would merely be retreating from one paradox to another: if it is absurd to talk of a reason for adopting one account rather than another, it can hardly be any consolation to us to know that one account (albeit unstatable) is the correct account. If one is to discard the categories of intentional behaviour, then one discards consolation. It is reasonable to find consolation in certain things, unreasonable to find it in others; being consoled is as much a rational, intentional activity as talking, driving, or reading a newspaper. Thus the first physicalist reply is unintelligible in precisely the same way in which 'The revisionary account is true' is unintelligible. As far as the thrust of Malcolm's paradox is concerned, 'The revisionary account is true' and 'We may console ourselves with the thought that the revisionary account, though unstatable, is true', stand and fall together.

A second reply is more helpful and consists in denying one of Malcolm's assumptions, the assumption that the categories of intentional, purposive, and rational behaviour are necessarily excluded from physicalist accounts of the world. That is, the physicalist will promise us an extensional account of intentions, purposes, reasons. He will presumably interpret all intentional behaviour (including the use of language) in terms of a more or less complicated stimulus-response model. Even the apparently complex action of making a statement will be unpacked in terms of responses or possible responses to certain stimuli (e.g. the utterance of the noise 'rabbit' to the appearance of a rabbit or to the occurrence of a thought about a rabbit, and so on).[12] If the analysis in extensional terms is successful, then Malcolm's paradox disappears completely.

5. *Provisional Results*

Although with a certain amount of exaggeration I described the first three objections to physicalism as 'feeble', our examination of them has not been fruitless. The third objection in particular served to bring further to our attention the notion of intentions, purposes, and reasons. And the second physicalist reply to Malcolm's paradox—his promising to give an extensional account of intentions, purposes, and reasons—dictates the course of the next chapter. Recent philosophical discussion of physicalism has paid far too much attention to possible physicalist accounts of sensations, thoughts, sense-impressions, that is, of states of consciousness. As we shall see, by far the most crucial difficulties arise in possible physicalist accounts of intentions, purposes, and reasons. And if physicalism is to be comprehensive, to give us a complete account of persons, it must give a full account of their intentions, purposes, and reasons as well as their sensations, thoughts, and sense-impressions.

[12] Those who wish to delve into an extensional account of language in general, and 'rabbit' in particular, are encouraged to read W. V. O. Quine's *Word and Object*.

7

DIFFICULTIES IN THE REVISIONARY ACCOUNT

1. *Two Areas of Obscurity*

HAVING disposed of a group of three misguided objections to the revisionary account we are ready to plunge into a second group which constitutes a large-scale (and as we shall see, devastating) attack on the claim that the account is comprehensive, coherent, and physicalist. The first two objections consist in attempts to show that the account cannot be both comprehensive and physicalist; the third points out that the account is internally inconsistent. Each takes up a point or points that I have already made, but whereas I have been content to leave certain areas of the argument in obscurity, we cannot now avoid casting light upon them. Indeed it has been necessary to leave certain areas of the argument in obscurity to allow the physicalist to state his case. A too critical assessment of his account in its early stages would have brought our inquiry to an abrupt end, before more general philosophical questions could have been raised. I hope that in allowing the physicalist to state his case we shall be able to appreciate rather better certain features of the descriptive account with which it is competing.

Two areas of obscurity in the argument of the previous chapter are of particular interest. The first area surrounds the general claim that the revisionary account is a more economical *substitute* for the descriptive account, that it dispenses with a concept (or concepts) which is (or are) *unnecessary*. The physicalist continually emphasizes that his proposals offer more economical alternatives to the descriptivist's proposals: 'By treating man, including his mental processes, as a purely physical object, operating according to exactly the same laws as all other physical things, [we bring man within the scientific world-view] with the greatest possible intellectual economy.'[1] But we want to ask, Are we making a *false*

[1] D. M. Armstrong, *A Materialist Theory of the Mind*, pp. 365–6.

economy? The revisionary account may in some way be a substitute for the descriptive account, it may dispense with unnecessary concepts, but it is not at all clear in what respects it is a substitute, in what respects certain concepts are unnecessary. A brick makes a very effective substitute for a book if I only ever use the book as a door-stop; if on the other hand I use the book as reading-material, I will not regard the brick as a substitute at all.

As I have pointed out briefly already, the physicalist is not claiming that the categories of the descriptive account are *logically* reducible to those of the revisionary account. Indeed he is likely to emphasize that such a reduction would be possible only if the descriptivist acknowledged the discoveries of physical science. We cannot expect (he will say) a scientifically backward account of persons to have any logical connection with a scientifically sophisticated account. To argue that the categories of one account are logically independent of those of the other is to miss the point entirely. It would be worse than pointless to remind a physicist that statements about temperature are *logically* independent of statements about molecular velocity; if he can formulate an equation which will correlate temperature and molecular velocity accurately, he is more than happy to talk of molecular velocity where we should want to talk of temperature. Similarly the physicalist is not concerned to analyse the concept of a person (and related concepts) in a strict sense of 'analyse': he is at most concerned to offer a set of concepts which do more or less the same work as those which they replace. A candle is not the same as a box of matches, but one can set fire to things or find one's way in the dark as easily with one as with the other. The reducibility in which he is interested is a reducibility of *function*; one set of categories is 'reduced' to another in the sense that one is *functionally* equivalent to the other.

Since the function of something may be determined by various contingent conditions, these comments bring us inevitably to the second area of obscurity, surrounding the relation between philosophical and non-philosophical activity. There are presumably differences between our philosophical and our non-philosophical purposes, differences which have been hinted at throughout this book but not articulated very clearly. At the beginning of Chapter 4 I was at pains to point out the distinction between scientific and philosophical physicalism, and I might then have commented that scientific physicalism should probably be adopted for scientific purposes but rejected for philosophical purposes. This is essentially the general conclusion I wish to be able to draw at the end of the book.

But we clearly need a general account of the putative differences between our philosophical and our other purposes to maintain the inquiry, as follows. Given certain features of the world (including human beings) we find it natural or useful or important or illuminating to use certain concepts. The philosophical task is to examine both the purposes and the concepts, to show in general why we have the concepts we have. A revisionary metaphysician is concerned to point out inconsistencies and vacuities in our purposes, and to introduce new concepts if these will serve our (consistent and non-vacuous) purposes rather better. In the case in hand our non-philosophical purposes include describing human beings; our philosophical purposes include weeding out unintelligible or vacuous descriptions, suggesting more illuminating ways of describing them, and so on. The first-order exercise is to describe, the second-order to examine the descriptions. It is of course an important part of the physicalist's case that there is a great deal of continuity between the first-order exercise (of scientific investigation) and the second-order (of reflecting on the first-order categories). And he can draw on a number of historical examples to show how our first-order interests may affect our second-order. We have no philosophy of astrology or alchemy, for example, but we do have a philosophy of physics and chemistry.

2. *The Language of Action* (1)

Let us now turn to the first of the three main objections to physicalism—which consist fundamentally in arguing that the revisionary account cannot be both comprehensive and physicalist. The general strategy of the attack is to force the physicalist to retreat three times, to a position which is unassailable but trivial. For the rest of this chapter we shall be contemplating the three stages of the retreat; in the next chapter we shall draw the relevant general conclusions and consider the comparative virtues of the descriptive account.

The first objection is an invitation to examine a central part of the concept of a person, namely the concept of an action. If we are to understand the concept of a person we must examine the main properties of people. Since M-properties are common to the whole of (spatio-temporal) creation, this means in practice that we must examine the peculiar properties, the P-properties, of people, those properties which supposedly turn up for the physicalist faintly disguised as the ψ-properties of brain-parts. They include a large number of sensation- and perception-properties (the possession of pains, sense-impressions, thoughts, etc.) and these have really dominated the discussion so far. But they also include a large number of action-properties, and it is to these that we must now turn our attention. If the physicalist language is to be of any philosophical interest, it must find a place not merely for sensations and perceptions but also for actions. It must not merely leave room for sentences like 'I have toothache, am seeing a red tulip, thought about the war, remembered his face, . . . etc.', but must also leave room for sentences like 'I raised my arm, drove to London, went to church, offended Jones, lost the election, . . . etc.'

Some of the actions I have in mind are comparatively simple and can perhaps be easily incorporated into a physicalist language, e.g. raising one's arm, running, whistling, scratching one's head, yawning, and so on. No obsession with physics is required to unpack them in terms of certain very characteristic physical states or activities—not necessarily states of the brain and nervous system but of certain other parts of the organism (the arm, the legs, the mouth, the nails and the head, the mouth and throat, and so on). But others, more interesting and more complicated, promise a number of difficulties for a physicalist, namely those actions which involve reference to a person's role, to his acting according to certain rules or conventions. There are the actions I perform as a parent, as a member of a club or college or state; I may act certain economic roles, as consumer or producer, taxpayer or tax-gatherer; I act according to, or in breach of, legal or moral rules; and so on. These would appear to present difficulties for a physicalist because they all essentially involve the notion of a rule or convention or role. I say 'essentially' because we cannot articulate any of the actions concerned without explicitly or implicitly referring to the appropriate rules, conventions, or roles. If I describe a man as picking up pieces of paper from a wooden desk, I am not offering a *poor* description of his visit to the bank; I am simply not describing his withdrawing money at all. If I describe a man as kneeling in front of a table, and dressed in peculiar clothes, I am not offering a *poor* description of the act of prayer; I am not describing the act of prayer at all. This is, I take it, a fairly familiar point which does not need expansion. The point is briefly that, if I am to describe such actions at all, then I must refer to the relevant rules, conventions, or roles which give the action its special significance (which make it praying rather than kneeling or acting the part of a priest in a play, etc.). And prima facie it is impossible to give a physicalist account of rules, conventions, or roles.

To talk of the language of actions is necessarily to talk of the language of intentions. Indeed one might define an action very roughly but quite usefully as any state of the world one might intelligibly *choose* to bring about or choose to prolong. Movements of the heart or intestine, eclipses of the sun, earthquakes, are not normally called actions because they are not normally things I could choose to bring about or prolong. *Abnormally*, I might: I might take drugs knowing they would affect the movement of my heart or intestine, and it would then make sense to say 'He changed his heart-beat' (rather than 'His heart-beat changed') or 'He has contracted his intestine' (rather than 'His intestine contracted'); I might be able to generate enormous nuclear explosions in space or beneath the earth's surface, and it might then make sense to say 'He eclipsed the sun' or 'He made an earthquake.'

Of course, to say an action is any state of the world I might choose to bring about or prolong does not rule out the possibility of unintentional actions. There are many things I might intelligibly choose to bring about but the choice is not always exercised, for one reason or another. It makes (logical if not social) sense to choose to step on someone's toe, but I may none the less do so unintentionally, without exercising choice, on a particular occasion. And since we do not always make the choices we ought to make or would be expected to make, we have a very large variety of ways of assessing actions, as rational, deliberate, intentional, careful, premeditated, sensible, intelligent; as careless, foolish, irrational, unintentional, pointless, inept, inadvertent, involuntary, clumsy, and so on.

Again, the language of intentions, like the language of actions, seems to be essentially non-physicalist, neither to imply nor to be implied by any set of statements about the physical properties of physical individuals. If this is indeed the case the physicalist is in a rather embarrassing position. He claims that his account is comprehensive, that it is an account of all individuals and properties of individuals which can coherently be postulated. He must therefore *either* give a general account of the actions and intentions of (what are to him) complex physical organisms *or* show that the language of actions and intentions is entirely vacuous, that our moral, social, legal, activities are essentially a vast charade. He must *either* give a physicalist interpretation of the claim that people act rationally, intentionally, deliberately, etc. *or* show that such a claim is vacuous.

The second alternative may safely be abandoned. For example, the most tough-minded physicalist will surely want to claim that he has certain social ties (to his family, to his friends, to his compatriots, etc.), or that he has been convicted of a driving offence, or that he is unemployed, or unfairly taxed. Indeed, it is highly unlikely that he will describe the last three claims as merely moves in a peculiar but essentially vacuous game. He will presumably want to distinguish rational from irrational actions, purposive from purposeless behaviour, and so on: '. . . is there any reason why a machine should not have the sort of purposefulness, appropriateness, and adaptiveness that is characteristic of human beings?'[2]

So although it is perhaps over-sanguine in a philosophical discussion to assume that one's opponent is unlikely to expound an absurd point of view, I propose to be over-sanguine and assume that the physicalist will adopt the first alternative. Indeed, as we saw in the previous chapter, we can safely assume that the physicalist will want to say he is deliberately, rationally, though perhaps vainly, putting forward his point of view as the correct point of view. If his account is to be comprehensive, it must make provision for a description of the physicalist's philosophical activity; it must allow us to describe what the physicalist is doing and why he is doing it.

So we may assume that he will recognize that there are certain ways of describing human actions and that an account of them must (in principle) be given. We have already noted that he is not in any case making a strict reducibility claim. He is not claiming that the categories of the descriptive account are logically reducible to those

[2] J. J. C. Smart, *Philosophy and Scientific Realism*, p. 107.

of the revisionary account. He is concerned only to produce a set of categories which is *functionally* equivalent to the set they replace. But even this weaker claim looks very implausible when one tries to work it out in detail. I said that it is useful to regard the physicalist enterprise as having three stages: first, we notice that a certain 'physical' description is extensionally equivalent to a certain 'psychological' description; second, we claim that the physical and psychological items are (contingently) identical; and third, we dispense with the 'psychological' description altogether in favour of the 'physical' description (or some suitable 'successor'). When we try to formulate a physicalist account of action and intention, however, it seems impossible even to complete the *first* stage. That is, it would seem that there is not even an approximate extensional equivalence between each action-predicate and its proposed physicalist substitute. And if two expressions are not even extensionally equivalent, it is not remotely plausible to suppose that they could be *functionally* equivalent.

Consider the vast number of expressions we use to describe human action. It seems clear that the criteria for using them are often context-dependent, that is, it is the context within which certain events (e.g. bodily movements) occur, rather than the events themselves, which determine which action has been performed. Sometimes the 'context' will include certain rules or conventions of behaviour. Uttering the word 'Guilty' does not of itself constitute a plea of guilty; I must do it before a properly constituted court at a certain established point in the proceedings; I must be the defendant rather than, say, the court usher, and so on. Similarly—as Caligula was rather slow to observe—making a consul is not simply a matter of, say, uttering appropriate words. There are certain rules to be observed, which determine which things can be consul, which people have authority to create consuls, in which circumstances.

It is perhaps less obvious, but true none the less, that the context in which an action is performed, rather than, say, the fairly overt physical events involved, is essential to the most trivial, least rule-governed, actions. On the one hand many actions can be performed in very many different ways. For example there is an indefinitely large number of ways of insulting someone (uttering offensive words or noises, tripping him up, failing to send him a Christmas card, leering lecherously at his wife, throwing refuse into his garden, and so on). On the other hand, a particular physical movement may count as one of a very large number of actions, depending on the context. For example raising the arm may count as simply raising the arm, attracting someone's attention, conducting an orchestra, flexing the shoulder muscles, warning, threatening, silencing a heckler, starting a prayer, acknowledging applause, buying a table in an auction, buying a clock in an auction, buying a plate in an auction, adjusting a curtain, demonstrating a dance movement, and so on. To make matters more complicated, some actions involve no characteristic physical activity at all—for example failing to send a Christmas card, refraining from striking a delinquent child. And it is perhaps essential to some actions that they involve complete physical inactivity—for example staying in bed in the morning, sitting at a sit-down demonstration. Intuitively I see nothing wrong in calling cases of failing or refraining and cases of complete inactivity, 'actions'. They are all logically connected with our choices and intentions, and attract all the moral or legal consequences (censure, congratulation, punishment, reward, etc.) of other, more active, actions.

I would suggest that in at any rate most of these cases it is hopeless to attempt to pick out an extensional equivalence between any action-statement and any statement or set of statements in the physicalist language. I say 'at any rate most' because I think a physicalist could have a good shot at the last group, cases of physical *inactivity*. I do not see any very good reason why sitting down at a demonstration should not be described in physical terms as the *inactivity* of a physical organism. After all one of Locke's primary qualities was 'motion or rest'. However, I am more confident about all the others; no physicalist shot, however well intentioned, will do. One might perhaps try to argue that I have exaggerated the importance of the context in which an action is performed, that there is some feature common to all actions of a certain kind (or common to their context) which can be isolated. If there weren't such a feature (it might be said) it is very difficult to see why we should talk of actions *of a certain kind* at all. If there were not something common to all cases of insulting, for example, it is difficult to see why we should call them all cases of insulting. It is not enough to shift attention (as I have done) from certain physical components of an action to the context within which it is performed; at most the shift of attention would suggest that the characteristic features of the action are to be found in the context rather than in, say, any appropriate bodily movements.

But of course this observation is beside the point. No one would deny that all cases of, say, insulting have something in common: what they have in common is that they are all cases of insulting. It may be very general and very trivial to say so but the generality and triviality are only to be expected. One cannot expect to find a very interesting and *specific* feature common to all cases of insulting. So one is not denying, trivially, that all cases of insulting have something fairly general in common. One is rather denying that all cases of insulting share a feature which *can be articulated in a physicalist language*. If there *is* such a feature, which *can* be articulated in a physicalist language, then we shall be able to complete the first stage of the physicalist enterprise (that of establishing an extensional equivalence between action-statements and physicalist statements); if not, not. And if we return to the examples I used, I would urge that it is difficult to see what feature common to all cases of, say, insulting could be articulated in a physicalist language. Since some insults involve some physical movements, some involve others, and some involve none at all, there appears to be no such feature. One cannot even appeal to the way in which the insult is taken. One might argue that the common feature is the way the action is interpreted by the person insulted. But this will not do, for some people feel insulted when no insulting action has been performed and others fail to notice when they have been insulted.

There is perhaps another possible move for the physicalist. Let us reflect again on extensional definitions. These are for technical reasons very common in mathematics. We might for example define 'prime number less than 20' as '2 or 3 or 5 or 7 or 11 or 13 or 17 or 19'. Such a disjunction is extensionally equivalent to the definiendum 'prime number less than 20' and, as far as it goes, is a perfectly adequate definition of it. Now the physicalist might make the same sort of move with action-statements; he might offer a disjunction of statements extensionally equivalent to the statement in which we are interested. And the disjunction would articulate every condition or set of conditions which could in appropriate circumstances count as that action's being performed. So 'Smith has insulted Brown' will be equivalent to something of the form 'Smith uttered offensive words or noises to Brown *or* tripped up Brown *or* leered lecherously at Mrs. Brown *or* . . . etc.' And then of course each of the disjuncts will be unpacked in physicalist terms, in terms of the states and activities of certain physical organisms and, in particular, of their brains and nervous systems.

So far, perhaps, so good. But this is really not far enough. Even supposing that 'Smith uttered offensive words or noises *or* tripped up Brown *or* . . . etc.' can be expressed in physicalist terms, we encounter a further difficulty. The physicalist is claiming that his language will be functionally equivalent to the language it is replacing, that is, the descriptivist language of actions, intentions, and so on. And the first stage of his enterprise consists in providing for every expression in one language an extensionally equivalent expression from the other. But if, as seems to be the case, such extensionally equivalent expressions in the physicalist language turn out to be indefinitely long, even perhaps infinitely long, it becomes highly implausible to suppose that they are functionally equivalent. In a very obvious sense of 'function' the language of infinite disjunctions would not function at all. No doubt we could develop a shorthand way of referring to all the possible ways of insulting someone. But shorthand is useless unless it can be cashed from time to time into longhand; and a longhand of infinite disjunctions would be too long for purely functional purposes. Or to put the matter rather more plainly, a longhand of infinite disjunctions would be entirely useless, however elegant the shorthand.

3. *The Language of Action* (2)

Before drawing any general conclusions I want to examine a possible physicalist account of intentions. The enterprise is the same as that of the previous section (to offer a set of physicalist statements extensionally equivalent to intention-statements, as the first stage of a thoroughgoing physicalism) and my criticisms will be very similar to those I have already offered. The account I propose to consider is to be found in Chapters 7 and 8 of Armstrong's *Materialist Theory of the Mind*. It is of particular interest for two reasons: first, as I have already observed, the language of action is also the language of intention, and intentions prima facie present formidable difficulties to a physicalist. Second, Armstrong makes use of a very interesting notion, that of a dispositional state, in an attempt to resurrect a discredited account of the will: 'It is the simple and natural view that my raising my arm is distinguished from the mere rising of my arm by the fact that, in the former case, my arm rises as a causal result of a certain sort of antecedent in my mind. When my arm merely rises *this* sort of causal antecedent is lacking.'[3] I say 'discredited account of the will' because of course it looks very much like the old and popular view that intentions are essentially mental causes ('volitions') which generate certain overt, usually physical, effects. It looks as though Armstrong's view differs only in the observation that such mental antecedents of overt physical behaviour may be influenced by a number of circumstances: 'To put forward a slogan: a purpose is an information-sensitive mental cause.'[4] Thus, just as a homing rocket will react in various ways to possible and actual obstacles in an attempt to reach its target, so a person will react in various ways to obstacles in an attempt to execute an intention.

But we (and least of all Armstrong) should not exaggerate the similarity between the old causal theory of intentions (demolished by Ryle in *The Concept of Mind*) and Armstrong's account, for there is one crucial difference between them. Armstrong wants to insist that the mental causes of our intentional behaviour—that is, our intentions—are essentially *dispositional* states of the brain and nervous system. When I form an intention to do something my brain and nervous system are in a certain dispositional state, a state apt under appropriate conditions to cause certain kinds of behaviour. The point of introducing dispositions here is 'that we can attribute them to objects even at times when the circumstances in which the object manifests its dispositions do not obtain'.[5] Now the account of intentions which was Ryle's target in *The Concept of Mind* did not treat intentions (or 'volitions') as dispositions at all, but rather as events identified as occurring at particular times. Indeed Ryle's suggested alternative consisted in treating intentions as dispositions, dispositions to react in certain ways to certain stimuli. So despite all the talk of mental causes Armstrong's position is much closer to Ryle's than to the position Ryle was attacking. The only substantial difference between Ryle and Armstrong would seem to be that Ryle wanted to attribute the dispositions to people whereas Armstrong wishes to attribute them to brains.

³ Op. cit., p. 132.   ⁴ Ibid., p. 139.   ⁵ Ibid., p. 86.

Thus, to sum up, Armstrong wishes to reduce intentions, purposes, motives, to dispositional mental states; given the general thesis of materialism, this claim collapses into the claim that intentions, purposes, motives are states of the brain and nervous system apt to bring about certain kinds of behaviour. And the most striking difference between intentions and other kinds of mental state is that intentions seem to respond to changes in stimuli, to changes in the agent's beliefs: '. . . the will is an *information-sensitive* mental cause: a mental cause whose operation is controlled by what the agent believes to be the case.'[6] And so by talking of *dispositions* rather than *events* as mental causes of intentional behaviour Armstrong avoids the objections which demolish the more traditional causal account of intentions.

We must now consider whether there are any other objections to which he is laid open. One objection might be that he has no right to talk of dispositions as causes, but since it is not central to our discussion I have no wish to discuss it here.[7] I wish rather to consider whether Armstrong's account of intentions will do as the first stage of a thoroughgoing physicalism about intentions, whether he has given us adequate material to articulate for each intention-expression a physicalist expression which is extensionally equivalent. Certainly the *general* account seems promising: 'I intend to do such-and-such' is presumably extensionally equivalent to 'My brain is in an information-sensitive state apt to bring about certain behaviour in certain circumstances.' But if the account is to be any use at all, it must in principle offer us a way of identifying *specific* intentions, *specific* motives, *specific* purposes. It must in principle yield an expression extensionally equivalent to 'I intend to become Prime Minister', one extensionally equivalent to 'I deliberately failed to send him a Christmas card', one to 'My purpose was to blow up the Bank of England', and so on. We must be able to find a set of physical conditions (including dispositions) which are characteristic of or peculiar to intending to be Prime Minister, a set which are characteristic of or peculiar to deliberately failing to send a Christmas card, a set characteristic of or peculiar to having the destruction of the Bank as one's purpose, and so on. If we cannot do this we cannot list our sets of

[6] Ibid., p. 150.
[7] It has been discussed in papers by Squires, Stevenson, Coder, and Armstrong, in *Analysis*, Dec. 1968, June 1969, and Oct. 1969.

extensionally equivalent expressions; we cannot complete even the first stage of the physicalist enterprise.

And for reasons I gave in the previous section it is difficult to see how we can, for there is an indefinitely large number of different ways of *intending* to do *x* or *deliberately* doing *y* or having *z* as one's *purpose*. Consider for example how many ways there are of telling, in context, whether a man intends to be Prime Minister—his words, his acceptance or rejection of high office, his willingness to work, his day-dreaming about 10 Downing Street, his rehearsing imaginary speeches to the American President, and so on. The physicalist is confronted with two alternatives, those I mentioned in the previous section. He might try to isolate a feature common to all cases of intending to become Prime Minister, or he might offer an indefinitely (or infinitely) long disjunction of conditions, each of which would be sufficient for a man's intending to become Prime Minister. The second alternative may be abandoned straight away. An indefinitely long expression in the physicalist language may indeed be extensionally equivalent to 'intending to become Prime Minister', but it then becomes highly implausible to suggest that one is in any way functionally equivalent to the other.

The first alternative, however, might seem more promising. Armstrong might argue that the feature common to all cases of intending to become Prime Minister is the presence of a certain dispositional state. And since dispositional states are identical with a 'categorical basis', i.e. with certain non-dispositional properties, we may conclude that the brains of all those intending to be Prime Minister share certain non-dispositional properties. Consider an analogy: we know that all glass breaks easily, is in the dispositional state of brittleness; and we know that dispositional states are identical with certain non-dispositional properties (a certain kind of molecular bonding); we are therefore entitled (rightly) to conclude that all pieces of glass, in so far as they are brittle, share a certain property (namely, their molecular bonding). No doubt by parity of reasoning we are entitled to conclude that there is a certain property shared by the brains of those intending to be Prime Minister which is responsible for their dispositional states, their intentions.

It is tempting to dismiss the proposal immediately on the ground that it involves assuming entirely *a priori* that there are certain properties common to all those intending to become Prime Minister, and that this assumption can only be justified *a posteriori* by scientific investigation. However, this dismissal would be inappropriate. At the beginning of Chapter 4 I made a very sweeping assumption about the amount of scientific information available to us, and Armstrong is perfectly entitled to make similar assumptions.

If the proposal is to be rejected it must be rejected for reasons already given, notably that it does not guarantee that we shall find a feature characteristic of and peculiar to, say, intending to become Prime Minister. It is not sufficient that we find a feature common to all those intending to become Prime Minister. It must be a feature which is common *and common only* to those who intend to become Prime Minister. If the guarantee cannot be provided then we have no way in the thoroughgoing physicalist language of distinguishing between an intention to become Prime Minister and, say, an intention to become Chancellor of the Exchequer.

The point becomes more clear and more plausible if we consider certain other examples, cases not of intentionally doing this or that, but cases of intentionally refraining from doing this and that (intentionally refraining from sending Smith a Christmas card or from shouting at a political speaker, and so on). And since the proposal under discussion was introduced by comparing the dispositional properties of those intending to become Prime Minister with the dispositional properties of glass, let us use the analogy of glass again, as follows. Glass has *inter alia* the dispositional property of not being inclined to burst into song, and it has it in virtue of a certain 'categorical basis', namely the absence of nerves, vocal cords, etc. In that sense the absence of nerves, vocal cords, etc. is common to all those things which tend not to burst into song. But it does not follow that 'having no nerves, vocal cords, etc.' is extensionally equivalent to 'tending not to burst into song', for an absence of nerves, vocal cords, etc. is also characteristic of those things which do not talk Chinese. So even when we have identified the categorical basis responsible for or identical with the dispositional property of tending not to burst into song, we still do not have a *complete* criterion for distinguishing that property from the property of tending not to talk Chinese.

By parity of reasoning we may find that all those who intentionally refrain from sending Smith a Christmas card share some dispositional property (i.e. their brains are all in some dispositional state). And no doubt this disposition has a categorical basis. But it is not at all clear that this categorical basis is *peculiar to* those who intentionally refrain from sending Smith a Christmas card. It is not at all clear that we have a *complete* criterion for distinguishing intentionally refraining from sending Smith a card from intentionally refraining from sending Brown or Jones a card. Normally of course we should use other criteria, other clues, to make such a distinction. In particular we should refer to many contextual details (the history of our subject's contact with Smith or Jones or Brown, and so on). But Armstrong has ruled out any reference to context, except in so far as the context has influenced the state of the subject who is intentionally refraining from this, that, or the other. Even taking such influences into account, however, it is difficult to see what categorical basis could be characteristic of and peculiar to those who intentionally refrain from sending Smith a card, and which would enable us to distinguish their intentionally so refraining from intentionally refraining to send Brown or to send Jones a card.

Before closing this section I wish to consider an objection to the whole strategy of my attack on Armstrong. I have been concerned to show that Armstrong cannot possibly complete the first stage of a thoroughgoing physicalism, for he cannot provide a series of extensionally equivalent substitutes for various expressions in the language of intentions. And yet I was at pains to emphasize the close similarity between Armstrong's and Ryle's accounts of intentions, the fact that both regard intentions as consisting in certain dispositions to respond to certain stimuli.[8] The only substantial difference is that Ryle attributes the dispositions to people, Armstrong to brains and nervous systems. But it might well be asked whether my attack on Armstrong is not also an attack on Ryle, indeed on anyone whose account of intention is fundamentally Wittgensteinian. Presumably Ryle cannot give a series of extensionally equivalent behavioural substitutes for expressions in the language of intentions. If he tries to find one feature peculiar

[8] Professor Ryle has pointed out to me that his alternative to 'The Myth of Volitions' is strictly an account of motives, not of intentions. And I would agree that there are certain important differences between motives and intentions. However, I would suggest that the account of intentions I have attributed to him emerges very clearly from Ch. III ('The Will'), Ch. V ('Dispositions and Occurrences'), and parts of Ch. IX ('The Intellect'), of *The Concept of Mind*.

to all cases of, say, intending to be Prime Minister, he will fail; and if he offers an indefinitely long disjunction of such features, he will be offering an expression extensionally but not functionally equivalent to the expression it is designed to replace.

But the question of design is all-important. It would indeed be embarrassing if I were committed by the attack on Armstrong to rejecting all Wittgensteinian accounts of intention. It has to be admitted that it *is* an attack on all radical behaviourists, on all those who wish to engineer a thoroughgoing behaviourism which is parallel in strategy to the thoroughgoing physicalism we are discussing. A thoroughgoing behaviourism would have three similar stages: first, one would notice that certain behavioural statements are extensionally equivalent to certain intention-statements; second, on the grounds of economy one would move from extensional equivalence to (contingent) identity; and third, one would dispense entirely with the original intention-expressions in favour of behavioural substitutes. My argument against the three-stage physicalism is indeed an argument against a three-stage behaviourism. Neither can complete the first stage.

But by no means all Wittgensteinian accounts of intention are thoroughly behavioural. A Rylean for example has no desire to remove words like 'intends' from the language. He is rather seeking to show where the *general* criteria of application of intention-expressions are to be found: they are to be found in a study of systematic responses to stimuli rather than, say, in a search for certain mental causes, certain 'volitions'. Thus a Rylean is not committed to looking for extensionally equivalent substitutes for expressions in the language of intention, and cannot be criticized for failing in the search. In short, my attack on Armstrong remains an attack only on those who wish to *reduce* intention-expressions to e.g. physicalist or behavioural expressions— 'reduce' in the sense that, were reduction completed, the intention-expression could be discarded entirely. But anyone who makes a rather weaker bid will avoid the attack completely.

4. *Intentionality*

The conclusion to be drawn from the previous two sections, then, is that the physicalist cannot offer a coherent account of actions and intentions. Indeed he cannot even complete the first stage of his three-stage enterprise. He cannot produce for every action- or intention-statement an appropriate physicalist statement extensionally equivalent to it. He may perhaps be able to produce an extensionally equivalent disjunction of physicalist statements, but since the disjunction is likely to be indefinitely, if not infinitely, long, it will hardly do the trick. So the physicalist might retreat to a much weaker claim altogether, namely that his account was intended to serve only a very limited range of purposes, those vaguely called 'epistemological'. That is, he is not concerned to provide categories which will serve every purpose served by descriptivist categories. He is concerned rather to provide substitutes for the epistemological categories of the descriptive account. He does not get better answers to all questions, for he does not get answers to all questions; but he gets better answers to some questions.

It is not clear what 'epistemological' is supposed to include or exclude. But as we shall see, since there are central difficulties in his argument, it is not important that we clarify the matter very much. It is at least obvious that he has no intention of talking about people's actions and intentions; he is concerned rather with sentences of the form 'X thinks about . . . , believes that . . . , knows that . . . , wonders whether . . . , perceives . . .', and so on. And he is interested in the thinking, believing, knowing, wondering, perceiving, rather than in that which is thought, believed, known, wondered about, perceived. Given this general restriction on his task, on the kinds of philosophical problem which he intends to clarify, solve, or dissolve, he continues to press the claim that the revisionary account is superior to the descriptive account as an account of the concept of a person.

Unfortunately a problem immediately arises, the problem of intentionality. It is a problem which has proved exceptionally difficult for philosophers in general, but it is peculiarly embarrassing for the physicalist. It is now accepted that at least some mental phenomena are intentional—indeed for Brentano intentionality was the distinctive feature of mind. There is a connection of a peculiar kind between a thought about Napoleon and Napoleon, between beliefs about fairies and fairies, between a sensation of heat and a hot object, between my searching for Atlantis and Atlantis, and so on. It is a peculiar connection, for one term connected may not exist. I may be thinking about fairies, unicorns, or round squares. And there is a corresponding philosophical problem, to give an account of intentionality, of the 'aboutness' of certain psychological verbs.

But perhaps to talk of 'aboutness' is to rush on too fast. Even to talk of *the* problem of intentionality is misleading, for there are many problems or versions of the problem. So let us note one or two of them and restrict the scope of the discussion a little. Many of the problems are discussed in §§ 31–2 of W. V. O. Quine's *Word and Object*, although, as we shall see, his main concerns are not ours. The problem (or problems) of intentionality is really a problem about reference. If we encounter a referring term in a sentence, there is a presumption that we can quantify over the individual(s) referred to; that is, there is a presumption that I can move from something of the form 'Fa' to something of the form '$\exists x Fx$'. There is also a presumption about substitutivity of identity; that is, there is a presumption that we can move from 'Fa' via '$a = b$' to 'Fb' *salva veritate*. Suppose Smith is fat and Smith is identical with the chairman of the Cricket Club. There is a presumption, first, that there is something that is Smith and, second, that the chairman of the Cricket Club is fat.

The problem (or problems) of intentionality arises because those presumptions are frequently defeated in natural languages. For example it is defeated in sentences of the form 'X believes that p', 'Y thinks that p', 'It is possible that p', 'It is necessary that p'. For some of the purported referring terms in 'p' may not be quantifiable, or substitutable *salva veritate*. I may believe that Mr. Pickwick is standing over there, but it does not follow that there is something which is Mr. Pickwick, nor does it follow that I believe that the man who was sued for breach of promise by Mrs. Bardell is standing over there. For the first conclusion would be false; the second may be unwarranted, because I do not know much about Mr. Pickwick. Similarly, it is possible that the number of Houses of Parliament is four, but it does not follow that it is possible that two is four.

So there may be problems with psychological verbs whose accusatives purport to be names or descriptions of *things*. (This the problems with which Quine is primarily concerned. I want rather to concentrate on problems with psychological verbs whose accusatives purport to be names or descriptions of *things*. (This means among other things that Quine's suggested solution of his problem is not an appropriate solution of mine.) We are concerned then with accusatives which purport to be referring terms, purport to pick out a particular thing or group of things. Where the accusatives do not purport to refer at all, there is no 'peculiar connection' (as I called it earlier) to be investigated. For example difficulties do not arise with sentences such as 'Smith is looking for a porter' or 'Jones is hunting foxes'. 'A porter' and 'foxes' do not purport to refer to a particular porter or particular foxes. That is, the sentences could not be analysed as:

'$\exists x$ (x is a porter and Smith is looking for x)'
or '$\exists y$ (y is a fox and Jones is hunting y)'.

I may look or hunt with no confidence that I shall find or kill anything. A more appropriate analysis would be:

'Smith is trying to ensure that $\exists x$ (x is a porter and x carries Smith's bags)'
or 'Jones is trying to ensure that $\exists y$ (y is a fox and Jones kills y)'.

In contrast, a problem does arise with psychological verbs (or verb phrases) whose accusatives do purport to refer. For example in 'I am thinking about Dickens' or 'I am searching for Atlantis', 'Dickens' and 'Atlantis' do purport to refer to a particular thing in each case (viz. to Dickens and Atlantis). Normally, as I observed, referring terms allow existential generalization and substitutivity of identity. But the accusatives of these intentional verbs clearly do not. The existential generalization test clearly fails, for we cannot infer '$\exists y$ (I am thinking about y)' from 'I am thinking about Dickens', or '$\exists z$ (I am searching for z)' from 'I am searching for Atlantis'. Dickens and Atlantis may not exist. And it is not at all clear that the substitution test fares any better. There is a sense in which, though thinking about Dickens, I may not be thinking about the contributor to *Household Words*, for I may not know of him as the contributor to *Household Words*.

Our problem then is to give an account of this peculiar purported reference to Atlantis, a particular unicorn, Dickens, the Angel Gabriel, and so on. To state that there is a problem is not of course to be committed to any particular solution. It is not to claim for example that the 'peculiar relation' between mental states and certain individuals is a genuine relation, or that it can (or cannot) be analysed extensionally. The descriptivist will perhaps welcome the use of the word 'relation', since he will tend to formulate the problem as that of explaining, or leaving room for, a peculiar relation between mental states and certain entities (or non-entities). And a possible solution of the problem might suggest itself: the descriptivist might regard the problem of intentionality as parallel to the problem of the meaning of expressions in a language.[9] Thus, just as he wishes on occasion to analyse the relation between, say, 'unicorn' and unicorns, he also wishes to analyse in very much the same way the relation between my thought about a unicorn and a unicorn. Just as we find nothing peculiar about our using 'unicorn' to refer to unicorns, so we would find nothing peculiar about our having thoughts about unicorns. We might even fabricate a verb 'intends' to correspond to the verb 'means' or 'refers (to)'; just as 'unicorn' means *unicorn* and 'a unicorn' refers to a unicorn, so a thought about a unicorn *intends* a unicorn.

But we are not particularly concerned to investigate possible descriptivist analyses of intentionality; we are concerned rather to examine the physicalist's proposals. It is quite clear that the physicalist will consider the problem of intentionality a problem:

. . . any theory of the mind must be able to give some account or analysis of the intentionality of mental states, or else it must accept it as an ultimate, irreducible, feature of the mental . . . no Materialist can claim that intentionality is an unique, unanalysable property of mental processes and still be consistent with his Materialism. A Materialist is forced to attempt an *analysis* of intentionality.[10]

Broadly speaking he may approach the problem in one of three ways, which we shall consider in turn.

First, he might argue that his physicalist account of persons must be supplemented by a non-physicalist account of intentional phenomena. The supplementary account will be non-physicalist, '. . . not because human behaviour involving "higher thought processes" is not in principle capable of physical . . . explanation

---

[9] This is the approach adopted (apparently with profit) by Wilfrid Sellars, in Ch. III of his *Science and Metaphysics*. It is by no means a new approach. It is reasonable to interpret a passage in the *Tractatus* as a suggestion that the intentionality of mental states is analogous to the meaning of expressions in a language: '5.542: It is clear, however, that "A believes p", "A has the thought p", and "A says p" are of the form, " 'p' says p". . . .'

[10] D. M. Armstrong, *A Materialist Theory of the Mind*, pp. 41 and 57.

and prediction; but rather because the problem is one of the logical reducibility or irreducibility of discourse involving *aboutness* (i.e. intentional terms), to the language of behavioural or neurophysiological description'.[11] That is, I can explain and predict the occurrence of my thought about the Golden Fleece in entirely physical terms; I cannot analyse the content of the thought (a sentence such as 'I am thinking about the Golden Fleece') in physical terms. To analyse that content I must employ a non-physicalist vocabulary, the vocabulary of *'aboutness'*.

This approach is fatal. If the physicalist supplements his (physicalist) account of persons with a non-physicalist account of intentional phenomena then his general thesis (that all individuals are physical individuals or properties of physical individuals) is false. To dismiss the problem as merely a problem about language is in effect to act as if people did not use language at all. If they do indeed use language and if their properties are all to be analysed in physicalist terms, then the language they use must be given a suitable extensional interpretation.

There is a further difficulty. The physicalist might be prepared to allow a certain logical raggedness in his account if it fulfilled other more fundamental requirements which he takes to be important, e.g. if it were scientifically realistic. But as a scientific realist the physicalist has use only for those individuals or properties that can be experimentally investigated. And many of the individuals which feature in intentional discourse (the Golden Fleece, fairies, unicorns, round squares) do not exist and cannot be experimentally investigated. A scientist cannot even in principle investigate the properties of the Golden Fleece, fairies, unicorns, or round squares in the way that he can investigate those of the table on which I am writing. So if the physicalist is to offer an account at all, he must offer an extensional account of such sentences as 'I am thinking about the Golden Fleece, . . . a unicorn, . . . fairies, . . . a round square.' He must argue that although there is prima facie a peculiar relation between certain physical individuals (experiences or brain-states) and certain other entities (or non-entities), an extensional account of the relation can be given, that secunda facie there is no *peculiar* relation at all.

So if the revisionary account is to be an interesting and serious alternative to the descriptive account it must include an extensional

---

11 H. Feigl, *The 'Mental' and the 'Physical'*, p. 417 (reprint, p. 50).

analysis of intentionality. The second and third approaches to the problem are both attempts to do this. Instead of talking about the intentional relation between certain experiences (i.e. brain-states) and certain individuals (the Golden Fleece, unicorns, etc.), we are invited to talk about the role which the experiences (or brain-states) play in certain human behaviour. The second approach is an extensional version of the descriptivist suggestion I mentioned earlier: intentional relations are regarded as analogous or even reducible to semantical relations.

Let us consider a particular example, a thought about the Golden Fleece. By using our new verb 'intends' we can formulate the analysandum:

(i) 'A thought about the Golden Fleece intends the Golden Fleece.'

The next operation is to eliminate reference to intending in favour of reference to meaning or designating or referring, as follows:

(ii) ' "The Golden Fleece" expresses a thought about the Golden Fleece and "The Golden Fleece" refers to the Golden Fleece.'

We are now, as it were, talking rather more about *meaning* and rather less about *intending*. We then detach the part which commemorates the shift of emphasis:

(iii) ' "The Golden Fleece" refers to the Golden Fleece.'

And then we elaborate an extensional account of meaning:

(iv) 'Among native language-speakers, whenever the Golden Fleece is observed "the Golden Fleece" is uttered.'

Presumably we then embark on a stimulus-response account of language. It may well be a very sophisticated model, of complex stimuli and rather complicated responses: after all, Armstrong wished to argue that intentions are information-sensitive mental causes, and our linguistic intentions will be sensitive to very complicated information.

So the general purpose of this approach is clear. That the purpose is not and cannot be fulfilled, is even more clear. One does not have to be particularly sceptical to be dissatisfied with the moves from (i) to (ii) and from (iii) to (iv). As for the first move from (i) to (ii), it is entirely unclear what ' "the Golden Fleece" expresses a thought about the Golden Fleece' actually means. All we appear to convey by this rather curious assault on the English language is that a certain thought is a thought about the Golden Fleece and that 'the Golden Fleece' refers to the Golden Fleece.

And that, one might think, is not a remarkable result. We have certainly not drawn a parallel between intentional and semantical relations sufficient to support the claim that (ii) will do as an analysis of (i).

But even if we were to ignore the incoherence of (ii) there are difficulties in the second move from (iii) to (iv). As usual we cannot complain that (iii) and (iv) are not logically equivalent, for the physicalist is concerned to produce an analysans which is *functionally* not logically equivalent to its analysandum. But one can cheerfully make this concession, for it is quite clear that (iv), however modified, is not even extensionally equivalent to (iii). For it is impossible to specify how many native language-speakers must make the appropriate response before we can reasonably say that 'the Golden Fleece' refers to the Golden Fleece and not to the Angel Gabriel, the Prime Minister, or $\sqrt{(-)}1$. We can imagine cases in which 'the Golden Fleece' certainly refers to the Golden Fleece, but in which some or many or even most native language-speakers consistently make the wrong responses whenever the Golden Fleece appears. Nor is it any good to say that by '*native* language-speakers' we mean those native language-speakers who speak the language properly. For we can distinguish proper from improper speakers only by referring to the rules of the language. Crucial, then, is the notion of a rule; but the notion of a rule cannot be reduced to the notion of a consistent response to a certain stimulus, because such a reduction leaves no room for consistently *wrong* responses to the stimulus. In short (iv) can hardly be (functionally) equivalent to (iii), for we can imagine numerous situations in which (iii) would be obviously true, (iv) obviously false. The native language-speakers are frequently perverse or fundamentally foolish and are wont to remark 'the Angel Gabriel' whenever the Golden Fleece appears. Less facetious examples are easy to find: in our own language, the rules for 'disinterested' are clear, but the responses of native language-speakers are frequently wrong.

The Golden Fleece, fairies, and unicorns also generate a further difficulty, even if one accepts the moves from (i) to (ii) and from (iii) to (iv). Since the Golden Fleece (as it happens) is never observed (iv) is vacuously true (or vacuously false). That is, it will be vacuously true (or vacuously false) that whenever the Golden Fleece is observed by native language-speakers 'the Golden Fleece' is uttered. It would presumably be a matter of some regret to the physicalist that the non-vacuously true (i) should be reduced to the vacuously true (or vacuously false) (iv), of such regret that he might be expected to modify (iv):

(iv) 'Among native language-speakers, whenever the Golden Fleece is . . .' *what* exactly? The only possible substitutes for 'observed' are themselves intentional terms ('thought about', 'learned about', 'referred to', etc.) which fail the tests for extensionality. (For example we cannot derive '$\exists x$ (x is thought about)' from 'a is thought about', for a might be the Golden Fleece.) So even if we allow that intentional relations can be reduced to semantical relations we find that semantical relations in turn must be reduced (at least in part) to intentional relations. The circularity is vicious, the second approach fails, and the physicalist must try a third.

The third approach might be adopted by someone like Armstrong. (I say 'might be adopted' because it is unclear, to me at any rate, what precisely Armstrong's account of intentionality is supposed to be. Throughout the first part of *A Materialist Theory of the Mind* we are promised an account of intentionality, but it seems to suffer the fate of the gentleman who encountered a Boojum:

> In the midst of the word he was trying to say,
> In the midst of his laughter and glee,
> He had softly and suddenly vanished away . . .[12])

It consists in the general claim that, since experiences are those states of the brain which are apt to produce certain kinds of behaviour, the intentionality of certain experiences can be analysed in terms of the behaviour they are apt to produce. A sensation of pain is intentional in so far as I am likely to bathe what I take to be the afflicted spot (whether or not it is in fact afflicted); a thought about Napoleon is intentional in so far as it is likely to cause me to strut about with my hand under my lapel or to set off in search of books about post-revolutionary France or to utter sentences in which occur expressions like 'Josephine', 'Napoleon', 'Wellington', 'Elba', and so on.

This ingenious proposal encounters very much the same difficulties as the previous one and is also open to many of the objections which I brought against Armstrong's account of intentions.

---

[12] Lewis Carroll, *The Hunting of the Snark*, Fit the Eighth.

For example it would seem impossible to offer sufficiently comprehensive, sufficiently detailed, analyses of each specific intentional proposition. There are far too many factors to be taken into consideration. I may for example tend to grasp my left foot in desperation every time I think of the problem of personal identity, but we should hardly suggest that left feet have anything important to offer for the analysis of personal identity. That is, the proposition, 'A thought at t is apt to cause that organism to grasp its left foot', is not a very satisfactory analysis of the proposition, 'A thought at t intends the problem of personal identity.' In the situation we envisaged, however, they would be extensionally equivalent. So, just as when talking about language we found nothing peculiar in the regular occurrence of misguided (linguistic) responses to stimuli, so in talking about intentionality we find nothing peculiar in there being a complete lack of connection between the intentional properties of an experience and the behaviour which the mental state is apt to cause. Indeed some intentional experiences may be apt to produce nothing whatever. We often have thoughts about rather recondite things (particularly in dreams)—round squares, centaurs, the Angel Gabriel—thoughts which are not apt to produce behaviour of any kind. So the third proposal goes the primrose way of the second and first, and we must conclude that the physicalist has failed to give a satisfactory account of the intentionality of some experiences. He cannot even produce statements extensionally equivalent to the statements to be analysed. The first stage of the three-stage enterprise once again cannot be completed.

5. *Chez Bultitude Again*

If this conclusion is accepted the physicalist must retreat to an extremely weak claim. He cannot defend the claim that his interests are broadly speaking epistemological, for he cannot give a satisfactory account of intentionality. Crudely he must claim that he gets better answers until the problem of intentionality is raised. I wish now to argue that he does not get better answers, to force him to make a third and final retreat to a claim which is not a philosophical claim at all. The artillery for this final barrage will be provided by reflection on a general difficulty in the notion of personal identity with which I wrestled (with only limited success) in Part II. I pointed out that we can put pressure on the concept of a person from two different directions—by trying to separate bodily from personal identity on the one hand, and by trying to separate mental from personal identity on the other. Indeed it was because it was possible to put pressure on the concept of a person from two directions that we needed a concept of a person which was logically distinct both from that of a mind and from that of a body. I did, however, argue that since we could exert only a little pressure on the link between minds and persons, mental identity played a rather more crucial role than bodily identity in questions of personal identity.

So much for a rather indigestible summary of one strand in a complex argument, although it will be remembered that my comments on personal identity at the end of Part III were rather suspiciously digestible. But what has all that, digestible or not, to do with the matter in hand? What has it to do with exposing weaknesses in physicalism? We can start to answer that question by repeating a point I have used fairly frequently. An account of persons should be concerned with those properties, P-properties, which tend to distinguish people from other material things—their 'logically peculiar' properties, as I have occasionally called them. Now some of those properties involve the occurrence of characteristic experiences, some do not. In particular, action-statements and intention-statements do not seem to ascribe characteristic experiences.

The physicalist's difficulties in the first few sections of this chapter have really been the result of overlooking that fundamental and familiar point. He has concentrated (with some success) on P-predicates ascribing characteristic experiences (e.g. sensation- and perception-predicates) and has neglected to leave room for those which do not (e.g. action- and intention-predicates). And his attempts to force the latter into the mould designed for the former (by interpreting intentions for example as information-sensitive dispositional states of the brain and nervous system) fail. So, in short, if the physicalist is claiming that he can give a physicalist analysis of *all* P-predicates, he is simply claiming too much. However, he might make a much weaker claim. He might argue that although it is impossible to give a complete physicalist analysis of persons (for some predicates refuse to be analysed in that way), perhaps it is possible to offer a rather limited, rather watered-down, concept of a person which includes only those properties which *do* involve characteristic experiences (i.e. characteristic brain-states). We leave out of this rather limited picture of persons the more complex properties (e.g. action- and intention-properties) and concentrate on those which clearly lend themselves to analysis in terms of brain-states (e.g. sensation- and perception-properties).

It has to be admitted that without further explanation this would seem a rather bizarre move. After all, there seems no point in persevering with a physicalist account of persons which admittedly excludes many of their most important and interesting properties. But in fact if the physicalist is making a bizarre proposal so was the descriptivist, for in Chapter 2 he was engaged in essentially the same sort of enterprise. He wanted to elaborate a rather limited account of people with the aid merely of Humean impressions and ideas, states of consciousness. To do so was certainly to ignore many interesting features of people, but the enterprise had an important purpose, namely to give sense to a number of rather peculiar cases. In particular it helped to give sense to the Bultitude case, which could be described as a change of bodies case on one condition, namely that one could analyse mental identity in terms of certain continuities between states of consciousness, experiences. So the point of the physicalist proposal will be very similar. In his case, however, he will want to insist that experiences and brain-states are identical, and that we can construct a limited account of persons in purely physical terms. Or to put it another way, he will want to insist that by restricting our philosophical ambitions a little we can make personal and bodily identity logically equivalent.

I want to show now that not even that very weak (and perhaps bizarre) claim can be upheld. Even if we confine our attention to, say, sensation- and perception-predicates it is not true that personal and bodily identity will be logically equivalent. It is comparatively easy to prove that it is not true, if we entrust ourselves to the gentle care of the Contingency Thesis on the one hand, and the Bultitude family on the other. First, the Contingency Thesis, which provoked a great deal of discussion in Part III but which I have deliberately ignored so far in this Part. The Thesis was that experiences and brain-processes are contingently identical in the sense that certain brain-parts with certain ϕ-properties will also contingently have certain ψ-properties. Although a brain-part will usually have one kind of ψ-property whenever it has a specific ϕ-property, it (logically) might have an entirely different ψ-property whenever it has that ϕ-property. Although it is pain-ish whenever subjected to a certain stimulus, it (logically) might be thought-about-the-Angel-Gabriel-ish whenever it is subjected to that stimulus.

So far, so (unremarkably) good. Now let us recall the severe and distressing changes in the lives of Mr. and Master Bultitude (and so presumably in the lives of their nearest and dearest). In the course of setting out the descriptive account I implicitly used an assumption which (it now appears) corresponds to the physicalist's Contingency Thesis, namely the assumption that there is a contingent connection between a particular body and a particular series of experiences. This assumption did not commit us to any particular solution of the Bultitude case. At most it made it possible and more natural to choose one solution rather than another. Described as impartially as possible the case was as follows: at a certain time, say in February, there are two people, X and Y, whose bodies are B_x and B_y respectively. In March, however, the person identified as the owner of B_x exhibits all the character-traits, ostensible memories, etc., attributed to Y in February, and vice versa. The March owner of the body of the February Mr. Bultitude exhibits all the character-traits, memories, etc., of the February owner of the body of the February Master Bultitude, and vice versa. I suggested that it was natural and plausible (but not necessary) to describe what had happened as a straightforward exchange of bodies.

Since the assumption that a particular body and a particular series of experiences are contingently connected is only a thinly disguised version of the Contingency Thesis, we can set out the Bultitude case in the physicalist language very easily as follows: the March ψ-properties of B_x (or rather the brain-parts of B_x) are very similar to the February ψ-properties of B_y (or brain-parts of B_y), and vice versa. Since we can set out the case so easily, the physicalist is faced with precisely the same problems which faced the descriptivist. But (and this is the crucial point) if he insists that bodily and personal identity are logically equivalent, he is unable to articulate the most obvious solution, namely that the case is simply an exchange of bodies. At best he could only remark on the extraordinary similarity between the March ψ-properties of B_x and the February ψ-properties of B_y, and vice versa. To take the more plausible step of saying that one person has exchanged bodies with another is to admit that the criteria of personal identity are *not* exclusively bodily. And in insisting that persons are and are only physical organisms the physicalist is already committed to claiming that the criteria of personal identity *are* exclusively bodily. We must assume that the physicalist attaches certain importance to the role of ψ-properties (or their 'successor' properties) in ordinary social relationships, and will therefore be tempted to drive a wedge between the bodily continuity of bodies in the case and the continuities (or rather discontinuities) of the corresponding ψ-properties. To resist the temptation is to be forced to describe the Bultitude case implausibly as a spectacular coincidence; to yield to the temptation is to accept that the concept of a person is logically distinct from the concept of a human body. And this admission of course entails the wholesale rejection of philosophical physicalism.

In reply the physicalist might complain that, just as the descriptive account can be rendered coherent only for a limited range of fairly standard cases, so the revisionary account should not be extended to deal with logically possible, but empirically absurd, non-standard cases. The reply is not to be construed as an appeal to a rule of philosophical etiquette, of the general form, Thou shalt not excessively embarrass thine opponent. We may rather expect the physicalist to point out that our language is bound to reflect certain purely *contingent* features of the world. It cannot be expected to make provision for all the logically possible states of affairs that might (but do not) occur. In his account of persons for example we are bound to rely on the contingent identity of reference of certain ϕ-descriptions and ψ-descriptions: 'The identification of the objects of this twofold reference is of course logically contingent, although it constitutes a very fundamental feature of our world as we have come to conceive it in the modern scientific outlook.'[13] The logical coherence of a certain set of concepts may depend on certain empirical features of the world. In particular the empirical probability of the Bultitude case is so small as to entitle us to legislate that the meaning of 'person' is exhausted by that of 'human body' and vice versa. Consider an analogy: it does not seem to be logically impossible for a table to turn into a white rabbit. It would certainly be peculiar, but not

[13] H. Feigl, 'Mind-Body, Not a Pseudo-Problem', p. 38.

logically peculiar, for tables to turn into white rabbits. And in an admirable search for logical rigour we might distinguish between tables and tabbits, between those things which are always tables and those things which are sometimes table-like and sometimes rabbit-like. For, we might say, the criteria of identity of tables are different from the criteria of identity of tabbits: for example a tabbit is always a tabbit but not always a table (just as a person is always a person but not always a baby). But suppose as a matter of contingent fact there are no tabbits; surely, we might say, it is reasonable to legislate that the meaning of 'tabbit' is exhausted by the meaning of 'table'. Since as a matter of contingent fact there are no tables which turn into rabbits, there is no point in making any provision for the possibility. Similarly (to apply the analogy) since there are no Bultitude cases, there is no point in making provision for them; as long as we have an expression like 'human body' we have no need for an expression like 'person'.

Thus the physicalist is not claiming that 'All persons are human bodies' is analytic, in the way in which the descriptivist would argue that 'All persons are human bodies' is synthetic (and false). In making that claim he would be guilty of equivocating with 'persons' in the way we examined in Chapter 6. He is rather recommending that, given our scientific knowledge, the expression 'person' as understood by the descriptivist should be removed from our language (together with 'tabbit'). The so-called difficulties with which the descriptivist wants to confront us never arise.

This reply though persuasive is inadequate. It is persuasive because it is undoubtedly true that our range of expressions is a function of contingent fact. For example the criteria of identity of persons are different from the criteria of identity of babies. But if babies never grew into adults there would be no point in having the expression 'person' in the language at all, for it would do no work that was not already done by 'baby'. 'Person' like 'tabbit', would be redundant. But if we examine the reply a little more carefully, it becomes clear that it steers round, but does not counter, the original objection. Consider two theses in the revisionary account, one explicitly stated and the other a thesis I attributed to the physicalist. The first was the Contingency Thesis. We saw how important it was to have two sets of expressions, logically independent of each other, to distinguish the ϕ-

properties of an organism from its ψ-properties (or the ϕ-properties which will be their 'successors' in Feigl's more sophisticated language). We needed two, logically independent, sets of expressions because we needed to express the *contingent* identity of experiences and brain-processes. Second, I attributed to the physicalist a general concern in social relationships with the ψ-properties of an organism (or their 'successors'). For our ordinary social purposes we are more interested in certain continuities or discontinuities between the ψ-properties of an organism than in the continuities or discontinuities between its corresponding ϕ-properties.

But these two theses are inconsistent with the physicalist's dismissal of the Bultitude case. In articulating his general position he is admitting that there is no *logical* connection between the ϕ-properties of an organism and its ψ-properties (or their 'successors'). But to make such an admission is to concede everything that the objector is concerned to point out. It does not matter in the slightest whether we use the word 'person' or some other word, in pointing out that there may be logical differences between personal and bodily identity. The objector wishes to acknowledge two striking facts: that the experiences of persons are only contingently connected with their physical characteristics, and that their experiences may play a more prominent part in social relationships in general than their physical characteristics. He does justice to these facts by distinguishing persons from bodies. But the physicalist has done precisely the same thing, without using the expression 'person'. He has admitted that the connection between the ϕ- and ψ-properties of an organism is contingent, and he has admitted the greater prominence in social relationships in general of the ψ-properties. Like the descriptivist, and our hypothetical objector, he needs a way of acknowledging that certain continuities in the ϕ-properties of an organism may (logically) cut right across certain continuities in its ψ-properties. His reluctance to use the word 'person' should not mislead us; however we label the concession, it has already been made. The physicalist has implicitly deliberately left room for the Bultitude case, but has tried to confuse us by using a new set of labels.

6. *A Suspicion*

Keats, it appears, was of the opinion that philosophy will clip an angel's wings. Although it would be arrogant to make such elevated claims for the arguments of this chapter (particularly since he was referring to natural philosophy) we might perhaps be inclined to think that we have driven the physicalist to a very tenuous position indeed. He could not produce a coherent physicalist analysis of action- and intention-predicates; he could not cope with the problem of intentionality; and finally, even when we allowed him to try to construct a physicalist concept of a person which deliberately confined itself to Humean materials (sensations and perceptions), he failed. The Bultitude case was not perhaps of great significance in itself. It was merely introduced to illustrate the main point that a physicalist committed to the Contingency Thesis cannot claim that bodily and personal identity are logically equivalent. However much he tinkers with labels, if he is committed to the Contingency Thesis he is committed to claiming that there are criteria of personal identity (the possession of characteristic ψ-properties) which are *logically* independent of bodily criteria (the possession of characteristic ϕ-properties). If he insists that bodily and personal identity are logically equivalent he cannot articulate the Contingency Thesis; nor therefore can he even start his physicalist analysis of persons.

One striking feature of his whole account from Chapter 4 onwards has been the constant reference, explicit or implicit, to the scientific uses of our concepts, to the apparent need for a conceptual economy which will reflect the aims and purposes of the scientist in his investigation of the contingent features of the world. Bearing in mind my careful distinction (in Chapter 4) between scientific and philosophical theses, between scientific and philosophical purposes, we should begin to suspect very strongly that the fundamental weakness of physicalism is the urge to obliterate the boundaries between science and philosophy. I propose to indulge the suspicion in a new chapter.

8

SCIENCE AND PHILOSOPHY: THE DESCRIPTIVE ACCOUNT

1. *From the Specific to the General*

IN the previous two chapters we have been concerned mainly with a series of specific objections to the physicalist's proposals, and I have suggested that the last three in the series are, both severally and collectively, devastating. But we may cherish certain doubts, a certain suspicion that perhaps the rejection of physicalism has been just a little too glib, just a little too neat. And whether we remain generally sympathetic or generally unsympathetic towards physicalism, we may feel that there is still very much more to be said before the inquiry can be regarded as complete. On the one hand we may still feel (albeit rather vaguely) that there is something basically right about physicalism and that its advantages have been ignored, its disadvantages exaggerated. On the other hand we may suspect that a philosopher who lays himself open to objections as crucial and as devastating as those we examined in the previous chapter must either have mis-stated his position or have been misled by certain very general and obscure assumptions which have still to be examined.

In this chapter I propose to examine the second alternative, as being the more fruitful. That is, I propose to argue that certain general features of the revisionary account, so general and so obscure that the physicalist rarely acknowledges them, are the source of his more specific difficulties and that, once they have been revealed, we should feel no temptation at all to accept his proposals. The exercise is not of course merely therapeutic, for the results of the investigation will enable us to appreciate the comparative virtues of the descriptive account. It will appear that the descriptive account fulfils important philosophical requirements which the revisionary account fails to fulfil, requirements so obscure that perhaps neither the descriptivist nor the physicalist has even considered the problem of their fulfilment.

2. *Analysis*

We might begin our examination of the neighbouring bushes by reflecting on the notion of analysis. To do so is to a great extent to cover ground already trodden in previous chapters, but the points already made will certainly bear repetition. Presumably we are being offered two analyses of certain concepts, the concept of a person, of an experience, of a body etc. One is a descriptive, one a revisionary, analysis. But it might be suggested that it is grossly misleading to regard the revisionary account as analysis at all. And of course if it cannot pretend to be philosophical analysis we shall be justified in rejecting it.

It is important to remember what is *not* being suggested. As I pointed out in the previous chapter it is *not* being suggested that revisionary 'analysis' is extensional, that descriptive analysis is intensional, and that extensional 'analyses' do not count as analyses. Certainly, if we made that claim, the inquiry would be brought to an abrupt (and, for the descriptivist, gratifying) conclusion. We should for example trot out a standard objection to extensional 'analyses' of certain statements. We should introduce the following propositions:

1. 'For any period of time *t*, there is a rise in rum-consumption during *t* if and only if there is a rise in the number of American Presbyterian ministers during *t*', and

2. '2 + 2 = 4 if and only if Bertrand Russell did not reach his hundredth birthday'.

We should point out that according to an extensional account of analysis 'there is a rise in rum-consumption during *t*' counts as an analysis of 'there is a rise in the number of American Presbyterian ministers during *t*', for the two propositions are as it happens materially equivalent. By the same token '2 + 2 = 4' counts as an analysis of 'Bertrand Russell did not reach his hundredth birthday.'

As I pointed out, even if such an objection to extensional 'analyses' could be sustained, it would be philosophically fruitless. For however we choose to label the physicalist's proposals, the interest is in the proposals, not in the labels. To refuse to countenance any extensional 'analyses' at all is to refuse to countenance any revisionary proposals whatever. It would involve a rapid but unsatisfying rejection of an attempt to introduce the concept of combustion in oxygen, on the ground that it is not intensionally equivalent to the concept of losing phlogiston; or a rejection of attempts to offer a phenomenalist account of material objects, on the sole ground that 'there is a tree over there' does not mean 'If I were in such-and-such circumstances, I would have a stream of tree-impressions' etc. So we must allow the physicalist to introduce purely extensional accounts of the concepts in which we are interested. And he will be mainly concerned with a particular kind of extensional account, for he is concerned to offer *functional* analyses. The notion of reducibility which he uses when talking of reducing the descriptivist concept of a person to the concept of a macroscopic physical organism is essentially a reducibility of *function*.

So far, the notion of functional equivalence has received very little attention, for we have been occupied entirely with the more general notion of extensional equivalence. The burden of much of the previous chapter was that terms in the physicalist language are not even extensionally equivalent to the corresponding terms in the descriptivist language and therefore that the elaborate three-stage physicalist programme could not even begin. Indeed one might think that it is odd to talk of 'corresponding' terms if there is not even extensional equivalence, and that in turn it will be odd to talk of functional equivalence. However, I propose to press on regardless, for there are still a number of very important issues to be discussed. That is, let us suppose that the physicalist has produced a number of terms which he claims are functionally equivalent to terms in the ordinary descriptive language. All the terms in the language of P-properties will have functional equivalents in the language of brain-parts and their ϕ- and ψ-properties (including their dispositional properties). We have already examined one general area of difficulty surrounding the notion of extensional equivalence; in this chapter I want to examine the more specific area surrounding the notion of *functional* equivalence.

The point of the manœuvre, then, is not to generate fresh philosophical discussion for its own sake. It is rather to enable us to discuss at greater length a point made very briefly at the end of Chapter 3, namely that the descriptive account seemed implicitly to acknowledge certain general limits on our cognitive equipment. We can use descriptivist concepts despite (or perhaps because of) such limitations. If the physicalist is to provide a functional analysis of the descriptivist concepts he must introduce concepts whose criteria of application do not depend on our using highly sophisticated scientific instruments. They must be criteria which any human being, however scientifically naïve, can apply successfully. In short (to anticipate a little) the physicalist is committed to giving a functional analysis, in scientifically naïve terms, of the concept of a person; he is committed to being a non-physicalist.

3. What There Really Is

To introduce the notion of functional analysis I propose to digress for a moment. The point of the digression will, I hope, become perfectly clear as we go along. We begin by reflecting in a general way on the notion of reality, not as a prelude to an investigation of later Idealism but rather as an attempt to give a sense to questions of the form, Are there Xs? or Are Xs Y? Indeed, to make the discussion more manageable, it might be helpful to juggle with the word 'really', to attempt to give a sense to questions of the form, Are there really Xs? or Are Xs really Y? Of course one interpretation of such questions immediately springs to mind: they may be straightforward unsophisticated requests for information. If someone asks me whether there are really adults four feet tall, he is only asking me if there are adults four feet tall; if he asks me whether butterflies are really fully grown caterpillars, he is asking me to explain the relevant relationship between butterflies and caterpillars. The word 'really' adds little to the questions save perhaps to indicate the questioner's surprise, interest, thirst for knowledge, and so on. In this respect 'really' and 'is true' work in similar ways, if Ramsey's account of 'is true' is to be accepted.[1] For although the truth-conditions of 'p' and 'p is true' are identical, it is convenient to have a predicate 'is true' to enable us to emphasize, confirm, teach, persuade, and so on. Likewise, although 'a is F' and 'a is really F' have identical truth-conditions, the use of 'really' enables us to emphasize, confirm, etc.

In this rather innocuous sense of 'real' and 'really' there would be nothing particularly pernicious in the claim that scientists are primarily concerned with discovering the real (microscopic) structure of ordinary (macroscopic) things. If a physicist tells me that a chair is really composed of molecules, which are in turn really composed of atoms, which are in turn really composed of certain kinds of elementary particles, he is only telling me that

---

[1] Cf. F. P. Ramsey, 'Facts and Propositions'.

chairs are composed of molecules, molecules of atoms, etc. The expression 'really' serves principally as a warning that we should not be deceived by our senses into thinking that all the parts of a chair will be visible to the naked eye, or as a reminder that bits of the chair will look very different under a microscope.

So much for an innocuous interpretation of questions of the form, Are there really Xs?, or questions of the form, Are Xs really Y? But we might attempt to interpret them rather differently. We might for example start to ask questions like, Is there *really* water, or only *really* molecules of H_2O, or are there *really* water-slices, or *really* bits of waterness? More disastrously we might offer a series of alternatives such as the following: Are people *really* physico-chemical mechanisms or are they *really* rational, non-mechanical things? Are all their actions *really* causally determined or some-times *really* rationally determined? Are they *really* physical com-plexes or *really* macroscopic simples? Are human choices *really* choices or are they *really* the outcome of purely causal processes?

Clearly something has gone wrong, for the alternatives are not genuine alternatives at all. Whereas in the first, innocuous, sense of 'really', the occurrence of 'really' in a question suggests that the questioner is surprised at a certain very striking piece of informa-tion, its occurrence in a question in the *second* sense conveys merely that he is confused. The uneasiness which such questions provoke is not a feeling that they are unhelpful, that there are in fact no clear criteria for deciding whether a particular account of the world has revealed accurately and comprehensively what really is. It is rather that the questions are irretrievably confused, for reasons I sketched in Chapter 1 and Chapter 6. We can if we wish interpret 'What there really is', broadly and vaguely, as 'the world independently of our describing it'. This is the inter-pretation which yields the first, innocuous, sense of 'really', the sense which allows us to ask and answer questions like, Are there really adults only four feet high? Are butterflies really grown-up caterpillars? and so on.

In asking questions of the second kind we are shifting right away from the innocuous interpretation to something quite different. And the absurdity of the shift becomes clear as soon as we reflect that what *really* is (in any sense other than the first, innocuous, sense of 'really') is largely a function of the way we *describe* what really is. It is grossly misleading to suppose that the world comes to us in fairly obvious pieces and that our problem is to decide the most satisfactory way of describing the pieces. It is only by describing the world that we carve it into pieces. As our survey of the fruit-cake in Chapter 6 indicated, we may have a number of wholly different ways of carving the world, which we may employ on different occasions (or even simultaneously on the same occasion) for different purposes. I am not presented with a collection of water-molecules and invited to label them. The labels I decide to use will determine whether a certain bit of the world (in an innocuous sense of 'bit of the world') is to be regarded as molecules of H_2O or as water or as a water-slice or as a bit of waterness. Similarly I am not presented with people and invited to label them. The labels I decide to use will determine whether a certain bit of the world is to be regarded as a person or as a partially closed causal system; as a rational being or as a part of a vast closed causal system; as a physical complex or as a partly non-physical macroscopic simple. In short, questions of the form, Are there really Xs?, Are Xs really Y?, must *either* be taken in the first, innocuous, way as requests for information *or* be taken as asking whether we need sentences of the form 'There are Xs', 'This X is Y.' We must ask, Do we have a use for the concept of a rational being? (not, Are there *really* rational beings?), Do we have a use in certain situations for the concept of a physico-chemical organism? (not, Are there *really* physico-chemical organisms?). Questions about reality collapse into questions about the concepts we use, the situations in which we use them, the purposes for which we need them. Questions about what there really is in the world (in the second sense of 'really') collapse, or should collapse, into questions about the ways in which we choose to *describe* the world.[2]

Of course, the choice cannot be arbitrary. To be able to describe the world at all I must have empirical criteria of application of the concepts I wish to apply. It is logically absurd rather than practically self-defeating to introduce a distinction for which I have no empirical criteria of application. And these criteria in turn cannot be arbitrary. They will be determined for example by the comparative efficiency of our sense-organs, the breadth of our experience, the sophistication of our scientific instruments. Obvious

[2] For more pitfalls associated with 'real', cf. J. L. Austin, *Sense and Sensibilia*, Ch. VII, and J. F. Bennett, 'Real'.

examples spring to mind: someone who is colour-blind can have no use for a distinction between red, blue, green, etc. (save in so far as it is extensionally equivalent to that between ripe tomatoes, naval uniforms, leaves, etc.); we can have no use for the concept of oil-pressure or weight if we have no pressure-gauges or balances. There are rather less prosaic examples: someone who has no aesthetic sense can have no use for the distinction between the beautiful and the ugly, save in so far as he is echoing the appraisals of others, for he is unable to apply the distinction of his own accord; the Bounderbys and (early) Gradgrinds of this world are unable to tell the difference between sincere emotion and maudlin sentiment. Formally, all such people are unable to employ certain concepts, certain distinctions, because they have no empirical criteria of application available.

It is here that my comments about the innocuous use of 'real' and my comments about its non-innocuous use overlap. We have rejected the non-innocuous use in favour of talking about how we *describe* what there is, in which situations, and for what reasons. But clearly if my choice of certain kinds of description is logically a function of the kinds of empirical criteria of application available, the real structure of the world, in our *innocuous* sense of 'real', will place certain broad limits on the number and kinds of things I can coherently wish to distinguish. So far I have only considered, as it were, the limits set by the 'real structure' of the distinguishers (their sense-organs, experience, scientific sophistication, etc.), but the 'real structure' of what is to be distinguished is equally important. For example it would be absurd to introduce a distinction between the colour of 'red' things and the colour of 'blue' things if 'red' and 'blue' things were precisely the same colour. It would be logically absurd because it would be impossible to distinguish 'red' from 'blue'. Conversely of course the real structure of the world might resist too enthusiastic an attempt to assimilate widely differing things; it would be a very peculiar conceptual scheme indeed which allowed us no way of distinguishing between water and sulphuric acid.

4. *Two Images of Man Again*

I hope that the oblique approach to the fundamental weaknesses of the revisionary account has not proved too oblique. The main points I was concerned to make in the previous section are, first, that unless we use 'really' in the first, innocuous, sense (as indicating a request for information) all questions about what *really* is or what things are *really* like should collapse into questions about our use of certain concepts, certain distinctions; second, that to be able to use a concept we must have empirical criteria of its application; and third, that such empirical criteria of application will be in part a function of the real structure of the world, in the innocuous sense of 'real'. A fourth and equally unoriginal point was only implicit in what I said, and ought to be made explicit. It is simply that we may use different sets of concepts for different purposes. In particular, the set we use for scientific purposes may differ radically from the set we use for our ordinary everyday non-scientific purposes, for the two sets of purposes will be radically different. In our scientific moments we are concerned to produce the simplest possible account of the world around us, sufficient to allow us in principle to describe any event as a function of certain others, and to predict its occurrence. The general urge to offer a simple account of everything sufficient to allow accurate prediction is rarely a feature, let alone an important feature, of our non-scientific moments. Indeed to talk of having concepts for a *purpose* is a trifle odd when talking of our non-scientific moments. It is not that we do not *choose* to describe material objects as material objects, or persons as persons, for we could still ask whether it was reasonable or foolish to continue describing them in that way. It is rather that, if someone were to ask why we described material objects as material objects or persons as persons or chairs as chairs, he would receive a rather trivial answer, namely that they are material objects, persons, chairs. We describe them as such because they are such. It is undoubtedly an advantage of having the concept of a chair, that I can see chairs as chairs (rather than, say, merely as spatial obstacles), but it seems excessively pompous to commemorate the fact by referring to my *purpose* in adopting the concept of a chair.

So let us drop the language of purposes and talk merely of using different sets of concepts in different situations. And the fundamental weakness of the revisionary account of persons should now be clear: it offers us a set of concepts which will certainly be useful in our scientific moments, but which has no place in our non-scientific moments. The physicalist has, I think, fallen prey to the temptation I sketched in my comments on 'real', the temptation to think that a philosopher should concern himself with what *really* is. Of course he may not use the words 'really', 'real', 'reality', but I did not need to use them in my so-called comments on reality. The point was a point about all investigations of what there is or what properties things have. I used 'really', 'real' etc. in my examples to make the point rather more obvious, more striking. The physicalist, as I said, has got into a muddle about what it means to say what there is or what there really is. It is easy for him to slide into offering a purely scientific account of persons, since scientists are concerned with what there (really) is. Armstrong for example on the first page of his *Materialist Theory of the Mind* asks, 'What is a man? One obvious thing to say is that he is a certain sort of material object. . . . The question then arises: "Is man nothing but his material body? Can we give a complete account of man in purely physical terms?"' On the next page he suggests that the proof of physicalism '. . . must come, if it does come, from science: from neurophysiology in particular'. Similarly Smart claims on the first page of *Philosophy and Scientific Realism* that 'As I propose to use the word "philosophy" it will stand primarily for an attempt to think clearly and comprehensively about . . . the nature of the universe . . . philosophy is primarily concerned with what there is in the world. . . .' (I have edited out references to ethics, which do not concern us here.) And as we saw in Chapter 6, even Wilfrid Sellars, who is not a physicalist, refers to the scientific image of man as revealing what really is, as offering us various 'ways of saying what is the case'.[3] It is just as unclear now as it was then, why action- and intention-statements (statements of the 'manifest' image) should not also reveal what there is.

Once we have realized that the scientist is concerned with what really is, in an innocuous sense of 'really' (or of 'is'), and that the temptation to think that philosophers should concern themselves with what really is involves a completely different, vicious, sense of 'really', the temptation can be resisted; and so in turn can the slide into offering a purely scientific account of persons. We may say that the philosopher should be concerned to analyse all the concepts we use, in whatever situations, in our scientific as well as our non-scientific moments. But this is not to be committed to regarding any one set (e.g. the scientific set) as better than any other set (e.g. the descriptivist set). Indeed we shall be concerned to

[3] 'Philosophy and the Scientific Image of Man', p. 40.

emphasize that one set of concepts can only be said to be better than another *within a certain context*. The scientific set is clearly better for our scientific purposes; the descriptivist set is better in our non-scientific moments. The comments on the two senses of 'real' are of course closely connected with the comments at the beginning of Chapter 4 on the difference between scientific and philosophical physicalism. In conflating the two theses, and in conflating the two senses of 'real', the physicalist guarantees a scientific answer to a philosophical question.

The impropriety of conflating scientific and non-scientific categories will become clear if we elaborate the general features of the descriptivist concept of a person, and take up the discussion of intentional action where we left it in the previous chapter. If we recall all the action- and intention-concepts which we contemplated there, it is clear that it is not only natural but necessary to rest them upon a concept which is essentially the descriptivist concept of a person. For the things which perform certain actions, described as rational or irrational, intentional or unintentional, and so on, are in some sense logically primitive. Arms do not act, nor do legs or torsos, nor any combination thereof. It is the logically primitive person (whose arms, legs, and torso they are) who performs the actions. Just as a game of chess cannot be described at all unless we regard the pieces as the basic items of the game, so the 'action-game' cannot be described unless we regard persons as logically basic, logically primitive, items.

The physicalist will claim that nothing I have said or could say about the language of action could show that the descriptivist concept of a person is in any way indispensable to it. For, he will argue, the concept of a person, understood as a complex (i.e. macroscopic) physical organism, will be sufficient to support, sufficient to make intelligible, statements about the moral, social, legal, economic relations between such organisms. Of course he will admit that his proposal forces us to reject the general claim that all properties of organisms are physical properties, but at least the proposal will not involve introducing a new, primitive concept, the descriptivist concept of a person.

But if my comments on different uses, in different situations, of different sets of concepts are sound, the physicalist proposal is logically improper. Consider an analogy: suppose I am playing football. In a fairly obvious way the object I am kicking, passing, trapping, and so on, is an inflated leather and rubber sphere. Indeed that it is made in a certain way of rubber and leather and inflated to a certain pressure is necessary to its playing the part in the game which it actually plays. But within the context of the game, that is, given that I (and others) are performing certain actions within the framework of intentions, general purposes, rules, and conventions of football, it is strictly incorrect to describe the football as an inflated leather and rubber sphere. It is strictly correct only to describe it as a *football*, as something which has a certain role in the game, related to the roles of other items in the game (players, referee, touch-lines, goal-posts, etc.). Similarly, it would be strictly incorrect, within the framework of intentions, general purposes, rules, and conventions of chess, to describe a pawn as a piece of wood of a certain shape which is moved straight forward and is sometimes moved diagonally one square to replace other pieces of wood. It should strictly only be described as a pawn, which can capture and be captured, can be promoted, threatened, and so on, for all these descriptions implicitly acknowledge that the pawn is part of a rule-governed game.

Applying the analogy we see that, even though in a very obvious way the basic items of the 'action-game' are complex macroscopic physical organisms, it is strictly incorrect to describe them as such. Within the framework of general intentions and conventions within which our actions are performed, the physical organisms should not strictly be described as physical organisms at all. If they are to be regarded as fulfilling a certain set of roles, they must be described in terms of those roles or possible roles. The 'roles' may not be very formalized; they may not be as formalized as the 'role' of a pawn in a game of chess. Perhaps it would be better to talk of a 'context' rather than a role. So, to repeat some of our examples, we must describe certain physical events not as certain physical events, but as an action of one kind or another, of signing a cheque, of breaking a promise, of giving evidence in court, of buying stocks and shares, etc. Describing a set of physical events as an action, however, is to characterize them in terms of categories which are logically quite distinct from the categories of physicalism.

Now our physicalist clearly does not deny that humans engage in purposive, intentional, conventional, or rule-governed activity. Indeed Smart goes further and claims that machines might do precisely the same things:

Suppose . . . that there were a group of machines which were able to communicate with one another, for example by beams of light detected by photo-electric cells. Suppose also that these machines were so complex that they had evolved, or perhaps had built in to them, a set of rules of behaviour and a legal and moral terminology whereby they controlled one another's behaviour. Such machines could correctly be said to sign documents. Some of the questions which these machines might ask one another, such as whether a document had been correctly signed, would not be physical questions but legal ones. . . . The remark, therefore, that not all questions are physical questions is irrelevant to the problem of whether men are or are not machines, in the sense of physical mechanisms.[4]

Unfortunately it is by no means clear that the latter problem, as Smart conceives it, is a philosophical problem at all. He fails to realize quite how much he has conceded in claiming that machines might engage in purposive, conventional, rule-governed activity. He fails to realize that, if his fairy-tale were plausible (and it would seem to be so), it would be logically improper to describe the participants in the relevant legal activities as physical mechanisms. In a very obvious way they (and human beings) would certainly be machines; that is, for scientific purposes a physicalist language would be perfectly adequate to describe them. But as soon as we engage in logically more complicated non-scientific activities, it is logically improper to continue to describe them (and human beings) as machines. In terms of a slogan we might say: far from showing that men are machines, Smart has succeeded in showing that some machines are men.

The descriptive account makes explicit precisely the ability to play certain roles which is not logically exhausted by the mere possession of certain physical properties. We can now perhaps appreciate the full significance of two theses of the account—the claim that M- and P-expressions are of different categories, and the claim that the concept of a person is logically primitive. Indeed in pointing out the general weaknesses of physicalism, we have come full circle. Although one cannot be completely happy with the details of Sellars's two images of man, it is now clear what he meant when he said that the manifest image makes explicit the general features of things which, severally, have individual intentions and, collectively, a system of community roles and

[4] J. J. C. Smart, *Philosophy and Scientific Realism*, pp. 110–11.

relations. Neither the individual intentions nor the community roles and relations can be intelligibly stated, save within the manifest framework, the basic items of which are material objects and persons.

5. Games and Language-Games

Before pressing on it might be helpful to summarize the state of play. I began by talking about functional equivalence. I said that the physicalist language might not provide extensionally equivalent substitutes for terms in the descriptive language, but it might be thought to provide *functionally* equivalent substitutes. I then made what might have seemed a rather irrelevant digression into a discussion of what it means to ask what there is or what there really is. But the apparent digression proved to be very important for our understanding of functional equivalence. For it seemed that the physicalist is impressed by the scientist's interest in what there (really) is, that he has been mesmerized by 'is' or 'really' and their cognates into thinking that the scientist can offer us easier access than anyone else can to what there (really) is. But there is, I argued, no reason to suppose that our non-scientific concepts reveal any less about what there is than our scientific; indeed we *must* use non-scientific concepts if certain features of the world (viz. actions and intentions) are to be described at all. In short, the physicalist language is certainly functional, but in a very restricted sense: its function appears to be to restrict our non-scientific interests, to describe everything in terms appropriate only to the comparatively narrow interests of the scientist. As philosophers we must leave room for all our interests, not just the scientific ones.

However, we may expect the physicalist to reply to these criticisms in very strong terms. In particular he will point rather significantly to the analogy used in the previous section, the analogy between games and language, between our correctly describing chess, football, etc., and our correctly describing the actions and institutions of human beings. For it is easy, he will argue, to commit what one might call the Language-Game Fallacy, a fallacy committed by Wittgenstein and his disciples. The fallacy consists in supposing that, since language and games share many formal features, they must share all their important formal features; or to put it another way, it consists in refusing to ask the question, What does this sentence mean?, unless taken as equivalent to the question, How is this language-game played? Both disciples and opponents of Wittgenstein will of course recognize the controversy. The Wittgenstein of the *Philosophical Investigations* was at pains to prevent us from seeking the meanings of expressions, and encouraged us to ask in general which moves in which language-games were appropriate on which occasions:

Hence the term 'language-*game*' is meant to bring into prominence the fact that the *speaking* of language is part of an activity, or of a form of life. . . .
. . . 'We name things and then we can talk about them: can refer to them in talk.'—As if what we did next were given with the mere act of naming. As if there were only one thing called 'talking about a thing.' Whereas in fact we do the most various things with our sentences. . . .
. . . For a *large* class of cases—though not for all—in which we employ the word 'meaning' it can be defined thus: the meaning of a word is its use in the language.[5]

The enterprise proved a healthy antidote to certain traditional accounts of meaning, for to talk too freely of the meanings of expressions is to raise rather than solve philosophical problems. For example instead of having to explain the peculiar relation between language and the world, one has to explain the peculiar triadic relation between language, meanings and the world. Further the notion of a language-game helped considerably to clarify certain rule-governed, or convention-governed, uses of language, the sorts of performative uses of language in which Austin and others later became interested.[6]

But to press the analogy between games and language too far is to court disaster. Indeed it is very easy to forget that it is only an analogy. (Whether Wittgenstein did or did not overstrain the analogy is a matter of considerable dispute, but this is not a dispute I either need or intend to engage in here.) For it is clear that there is still a fundamental difference between games and language. To express the point with a certain crudeness, games do not have and

---

[5] Wittgenstein, op. cit. I, §§ 23, 27, 43.
[6] Cf. e. g. J. L. Austin, *How To Do Things With Words*; J. Searle, *Speech Acts*, 'Meaning and Speech-Acts', and 'Austin on Locutionary and Illocutionary Acts'; H. P. Grice, 'Meaning' and 'Utterers' Meaning and Intentions'; P. F. Strawson, 'Intention and Convention in Speech-Acts'.

do not pretend to have any connection with the world; language does. In explaining the rules of a game I have explained everything there is to explain; in explaining the rules of a language I have not. It is not enough for me to say for example, 'Every time one sees a rabbit one should say "rabbit".' For the explanation to count as a complete explanation of the language, I must go on to explain that there is a quite peculiar connection between 'rabbit' and rabbits, a connection rather more mysterious than the game of uttering 'rabbit' whenever a rabbit appears.

It might help if we distinguish between internal and external questions about a game or a language. Internal questions are requests for information about the rules and general apparatus of the game (or language); external questions are questions about the purposes or point of the game (or language) as a whole. Let us consider a few examples. There are obviously many internal questions I may ask about the game of chess, about the number and kinds of pieces, their possible moves, the aims of each player, the circumstances in which the game can come to an end. We can ask similar questions about football, croquet, etc. The information required will normally be found in booklets entitled 'The Rules of Chess', 'The Rules of Association Football', 'The Rules of Croquet', etc.

Similarly I can ask internal questions about a language. I can ask how many and which kinds of noise or symbol are used, in which combinations, and when. Some of the answers will give information about the grammar and syntax of the language: 'One can never say "Table quietly an whenever"' or (less dramatically) 'One says "You are", not "You is".' Some questions, however, will seek more semantic than syntactic information: 'When a rabbit appears, it is inappropriate to utter the noise "donkey".' And this semantic information may include remarks about the category-distinctions of the language: 'One can neither assert nor deny that stones are thinking about Vienna, or that Joan is a strong verb.' Thus, just as we can say of a game that certain moves are permitted in certain circumstances and not in others, or not at all, so we can say that certain moves in a language are permitted, others not, others not at all.

So much then for internal questions about a language and internal questions about a game. The parallel seems quite close. As soon as we consider appropriate external questions about each of them, however, the parallel breaks down. External questions, I said, are questions about the purposes or point of a game (or language) as a whole. Internal questions help us to see moves as conforming to (or breaking) the rules of the game (or language); external questions help us to see the point or purpose of having those rules, or perhaps help us to see how the rules are related to certain features of the world. Now the range of external questions about games seems to be rather limited. If someone says 'Why do you play this game, what is its point . . .?', the only possible answers would be of the form, 'It is intellectually stimulating, amusing, distracting, . . . etc.' It would be absurd to expect any information about what the game represented, or what features of the world were described in the course of the game. It would be inappropriate for example to ask whether bishops in chess represented bishops and pawns soldiers. Of course it would be reasonable to sketch the history of the game, to point out the obvious historical connections between the present game of chess and the structure of a feudal society. But the game would still be the same game, still be played for the same reasons and just as intelligibly, whether the historical connection existed or not. Within the rules of chess it is impossible to mate one's opponent if one only has a king and a bishop, and one's opponent a king, but it would be absurd to accuse chess-players of impropriety if one found historical instances of a king and a bishop engineering, entirely unaided, the downfall of another king. By the same token it would be absurd to criticize players of Monopoly, on the ground that stockbrokers never win second prizes in beauty contests; or to point out to players of L'Attaque that in fact sappers do not always destroy mines, or that mines do not always destroy everyone except sappers.

To repeat the initial, rather crudely stated, point, games do not have and do not pretend to have any connection with the world; language clearly does. One can ask many external questions about a language which cannot be asked intelligibly about a game. If I ask, 'What is the point of that rule of the language?', I do not usually expect an answer of the form, 'It is amusing, intellectually stimulating, . . . etc.' I shall usually expect information about those features of the world to which one might refer when obeying the rule. There should be a connection between certain pieces of the language game, as it were, and certain features of the world;

certain of the more important terms of the language must have a reference. I can rightly accuse a man of engaging in a vacuous enterprise if he cannot answer such external questions about his language-game. If scientists are to be believed, a number of language-games are clearly vacuous, e.g. the phlogiston-game, the game of astrology, of possession by devils. For there are no substances of negative weight, no cosmic forces, no spirits inhabiting human beings. If Lewis Carroll is to be believed, a large number of the language-games played in Wonderland and on the other side of the Looking-Glass are vacuous, for they break fairly fundamental laws of logic. But in all these cases, whether we are talking about simple failures of reference or failures due to breaches of the laws of logic, the point is still the same. It is just not good enough to say that a certain language-game is played; if the pieces in the game fail to refer to bits of the world, it is an entirely vacuous game.[7]

And so at last we may return to the physicalist, who might make use of these remarks on languages and games in the following way. He might concede everything I said in section 4 of this chapter. He might admit that the language of physics and the language of human action are distinct, and that terms from one must not be confused with terms from the other. He might cheerfully concede that it is logically improper within the language of action to describe a physical organism as such. But even if he made those concessions (which would involve a substantial shift in his position), he would still insist that I have not shown that the language of action, as understood by the descriptivist, has any sense, that it is any more intelligible as it stands than the vacuous phlogiston game or the game of astrology or the game of possession by devils. That is, I must ask and answer certain questions about the descriptivist language in general and the language of action in particular. I must show that the descriptivist language is in some sense connected (as the game of astrology is not) with the world it

---

[7] Hence the absurdity of Norman Malcolm's defence of a certain theological language-game: 'Here is expressed the idea of the necessary existence and eternity of God, an idea that is essential to the Jewish and Christian religions. In those complex systems of thought, those "language-games", God has the status of a necessary being. . . . Here we must say with Wittgenstein "This language-game is played!" . . .' ('Anselm's Ontological Arguments', p. 56). And one must also say that, since the Ontological Argument is invalid, it is a very silly language-game.

purports to describe. If I cannot do that, then I must abandon it in favour of the scientifically sophisticated physicalist substitute. The substitute may not reproduce the complexity of that which it replaces, but that is after all only to be expected as we move from the scientifically naïve to the scientifically sophisticated.

As I remarked parenthetically, this suggestion involves a substantial shift in the physicalist's position, away for example from the position expressed by Smart in the previous section, in the quotation taken from pp. 110–11 of *Philosophy and Scientific Realism*. He has never before asked for any comprehensive justification of the language of action; nor has he insisted that *all* the concepts of that language (including the legal concepts to which Smart referred) should be forced into a physicalist mould. But having noted that there is a shift of position, let us move on to the more important business of discussing the new position, the attempt to assimilate the scientifically naïve descriptivist language to the scientifically naïve languages of phlogiston, cosmic forces, and devils.

As I pointed out briefly at the end of Chapter 3, the purely epistemological component of the descriptivist language presents no problem here. Since our need and ability to use a concept depend on our having empirical criteria of its application, it is easy to see why we use the descriptivist rather than the physicalist concepts of experience. Since we usually confront the world without the aid of scientific instruments, we usually need comparatively unsophisticated concepts of experience, concepts which are independent of the scientific concepts which the physicalist is trying to thrust upon us. We can distinguish tables from chairs, but not one table-molecule from another table-molecule. We can distinguish red things from blue things, but cannot (by means of our senses) measure wavelengths of light. I can tell whether I am thinking, whether you are in pain, whether Smith is depressed, whether Jones can hear the radio, but may know nothing about the human brain and nervous system. To use physicalist concepts of experience, however, is to use concepts which have physiological criteria of application, that is, it is to use concepts which many of us can never apply. It is surely a most striking advantage of descriptivist concepts, that they can be applied.

It is by no means as easy to justify our use of action-concepts— the language of reasons, intentions, deliberations, etc. It is tempting to treat them in precisely the same way I treated the concepts of experience. That is, we might begin by establishing to everyone's satisfaction that the physicalist and descriptivist action-concepts are mutually logically independent. We should then point out that concepts must have criteria of application, and conclude that an excellent reason for preferring descriptivist action-concepts is that they are tailor-made for the scientifically ignorant. The great thing about them, we might say, is that we can use them, however little we may know about brains and nervous systems. Regrettably it is a temptation to be avoided. The physicalist will point out that convenience is not of itself a very great advantage. The scientifically ignorant could and did play the phlogiston game, the game of astrology and of possession by devils, but there were none the less excellent reasons for abandoning them. We must offer rather better reasons for continuing to use descriptivist action-concepts. Or to put the same point rather differently, we must show that there is a vital difference between the language-game of action on the one hand, and the phlogiston-game, the game of astrology, and the game of possession by devils on the other, that the former is reputable in a way in which the latter were not.

There are really three points to be made about the descriptivist language of action, three points which add up to quite a strong reason for our preferring it to any physicalist alternative. The first two points involve a careful examination of the remarks about the phlogiston-game, the game of astrology and the game of possession by devils. Such an examination reveals that they are very different in certain important ways from the descriptivist language to which they are being compared. The first difference is that (at least in two of the three cases) the scientifically naïve language could be replaced *salva veritate* by an extensionally equivalent scientifically sophisticated language. Expressions referring to the loss of phlogiston could be replaced *salva veritate* by extensionally equivalent expressions referring to the formation of oxygen compounds by combustion; expressions referring to possession by devils, by extensionally equivalent expressions referring to various psychiatric disorders. In that respect at least there was nothing to prevent our abandoning the old languages in favour of the new. However, when we discussed objections to physicalism in the previous chapter we saw that there certainly was something to prevent our abandoning the descriptivist language in favour of the physicalist, namely that physicalist expressions were not even extensionally equivalent to the descriptivist expressions they were designed to replace. The move from descriptivism to physicalism is by no means a simple move from the scientifically naïve to the scientifically sophisticated.

There is a second reason for rejecting the comparison between the descriptive language and the language of phlogiston and so forth. There is no point in continuing to talk of substances of negative weight if it is impossible to isolate them, to distinguish their chemical properties from those of other substances; there is no point in talking of cosmic forces if it is impossible to identify them, measure them; it is absurd to talk of possession by devils if the devils can never be counted, located, or otherwise identified. In short, it is intelligible and desirable to abandon the scientifically naïve languages we have been considering, to insist that they are vacuous on entirely experimental grounds. If no one can undertake to provide me with a sample of phlogiston or to measure a cosmic force or to lock up a devil or two, it is worse than useless to talk about them. But none of this is true of the descriptivist language. There are fairly clear criteria for identifying people, states of consciousness, actions, intentions, and so on; no one can seriously insist on experimental grounds that there are no such things. Whatever grounds we may have for rejecting descriptivism, they are certainly not experimental.

The first two points have been decidedly negative, attempts to undermine the comparison between the descriptive language and various scientifically naïve languages. The third point is rather more positive. It involves trying to show why we should continue to use the descriptive language, and in particular the language of actions, reasons, and intentions. Rather crudely, what feature or features of human beings make it possible and natural to use the language of action? The answer, I fear, is more than a trifle platitudinous, namely that we have a language of purposes because human beings are purposive. (A platitude is not of course necessarily a tautology, for if we were sufficiently perverse, we could refuse to describe purposive behaviour as such.) Human beings, we might say, are things which make plans, for certain reasons, some good, some bad. There are good plans and bad plans, good planners and bad planners; it is easy to see how we find a use for expressions like 'rational man', 'reasonable action', 'unintentional action', and so on. Some of our plans are of course of philosophical interest—the plans of Smart, Armstrong, Feigl, *et al.*, their planned responses to objections, and so on. If we are to commemorate these rather peculiar features of human beings, we must have a language of reasons, intentions, purposes. And if the argument of the previous chapter is correct, it cannot be a physicalist language.

6. *Concluding Remarks*

No very useful purposes are served in prolonging the attempt to reduce all the intentional concepts of the descriptive account to the concept of a plan. Nor is it necessary to elaborate in any detail the concepts themselves, for this is ground already well covered by other philosophers.[8] I shall bring the whole inquiry to an end by making two final points which I have hinted at or expressed on a number of occasions already. First, I have throughout attempted to draw attention away from the very narrow discussion of the relation between experiences and physical states. Frankly, if physicalism is merely the thesis that all mental *events* are identical with certain physical *events*, then physicalism is obviously true. Smart, Armstrong and others have offered quite enough evidence to show that it is true. I am even prepared to concede quite cheerfully that all dispositional mental states are identical with certain physical dispositional states (and so in turn with a certain physical 'categorical basis'). I can see no philosophical objections to our identifying *events* with *events*. My objection to physicalism is that it simply does not offer us enough. It gives us the truth and nothing but the truth, but by no means the whole truth.

The reason is this. Although persons are not Lockean bundles of qualities, an account of persons consists essentially in an analysis of all their properties—in particular, all their important P-properties, the logically peculiar properties which generate all our difficulties about minds and bodies. As we have seen, some P-properties (having sense-impressions, deliberately reflecting, having sensations) seem to involve (at least, if not entirely) the occurrence of characteristic experiences, characteristic *events*. The

---

[8] e.g. R. Taylor, *Action and Purpose*, A. I. Melden, *Free Action*, G. E. M. Anscombe, *Intention*, A. J. P. Kenny, *Action, Emotion and Will*. They do not of course always arrive at the same conclusions.

physicalist can cope very easily with properties of that kind: pain-experiences are identical with one kind of physical state, red sense-impressions with another, and so on. He can also deal fairly easily with those P-properties which do not involve the occurrence of characteristic experiences but which do involve a great deal of fairly characteristic physical activity (scratching one's leg, shutting one's mouth, brushing one's hair). For although they cannot be reduced to states of the brain and nervous system, they can be reduced to states of certain other parts of the organism (the state of the nails, arm, and leg, of the mouth, of the hand and the head, and so on).

Some of the more complex P-properties, however, defeat him, for they may involve neither the occurrence of characteristic experiences, *events*, nor the occurrence of any characteristic physical activity at all. (Nor do they even necessarily involve there being any characteristic dispositional states either.) These were the properties in which I was interested in the previous chapter (acting intentionally, with a reason or purpose; taking part in ceremonies; insulting people; refraining from certain things; and so on). In short, the attempt to identify experiences with brain-states (events or dispositional states with events or dispositional states) is philosophically pointless unless it is the preliminary stage of a more comprehensive account of persons. But the comprehensive account must include analyses of properties which do not involve the occurrence of characteristic experiences (events or dispositional states). So the restricted physicalist equipment which generates the preliminary stage, the Identity Theory, cannot support the comprehensive account. This all may seem very obvious, but it has been acknowledged by only one eminent physicalist, Armstrong. But as I have tried to show, his attempts to cater for the very complex P-properties fail, because the notion of a disposition cannot bear the weight put upon it.

The second point takes up again the fundamental inspiration of physicalism, the fundamental and disastrous inclination to conflate science and philosophy, to conflate scientific and philosophical problems. It is of course absurd to suggest that philosophers and scientists have nothing of interest to say to one another. Indeed there may be a considerable degree of overlap between the two disciplines, in the sense that scientists and philosophers may arrive at similar conclusions via different routes (and I am not thinking of Hegel's attempt to prove *a priori* that there are seven planets). For example both may deny the existence of God, one because he is an experimental scientist, the other because he is a logical positivist. Similarly, there are both *a posteriori* (e.g. inductive) and *a priori* (e.g. Kantian) arguments for the existence of a spatio-temporal external world. Moreover, advances in one discipline may encourage advances in the other: seventeenth-century philosophy certainly sharpened scientific method, seventeenth-century science stimulated seventeenth- and eighteenth-century empiricism, and twentieth-century mathematics and physics have provoked considerable advances in logic and epistemology.

In that sense, then, there is no clear boundary between science and philosophy; or, to put it more precisely, it may be difficult to draw the boundary in terms of the *content* of each discipline. There is no one class of propositions to be labelled 'scientific conclusions', nor a class labelled 'philosophical conclusions'. Nor is it quite true to say without qualification that the difference is one of *method*, a difference between an *a posteriori* and an *a priori* method. For on the one hand a scientist must make certain *a priori* assumptions (about what counts as evidence for example), and on the other a philosopher must make certain *a posteriori* assumptions, or he would be discussing the philosophy of astrology, wondering whether trees were immortal, and so on.

But having conceded all that, it does not follow, nor is it true, that a scientific account of the world will be philosophically acceptable. As I have pointed out already, scientific purposes may be very limited; they may only include a desire to predict accurately and economically the occurrence of any event. We may be able to do that with a very narrow range of concepts. The scientist may for example be able to predict accurately and economically the occurrence of any event in a human being without necessarily using the language of intentions. But it does not follow, nor is it true, that we should accept a scientific account of persons: 'This was a case of metaphysics, at least as difficult for Joe to deal with, as for me. But Joe took the case altogether out of the region of metaphysics, and by that means vanquished it.'[9] The physicalist has taken our own case, the problems surrounding the concept of a person, well out of the region of metaphysics, but has by no means

[9] Dickens, *Great Expectations*, Ch. IX.

vanquished it. We should concede that he has drawn attention to certain outstanding scientific discoveries, but we should not suppose that he has thereby justified a thesis of philosophical physicalism.

BIBLIOGRAPHY OF PHILOSOPHICAL WORKS REFERRED TO IN THE TEXT

ANSCOMBE, G. E. M.: *Intention* (Basil Blackwell, 1957).
ARMSTRONG, D. M.: *A Materialist Theory of the Mind* (Routledge and Kegan Paul, 1968).
—— 'Dispositions Are Causes' (*Analysis*, 1969).
AUSTIN, J. L.; 'A Plea for Excuses' (*Proceedings of the Aristotelian Society*, 1956–7).
—— *How To Do Things with Words* (Clarendon Press, 1962).
—— *Sense and Sensibilia* (Clarendon Press, 1962).
AYER, A. J.: 'The Concept of a Person' (in *Concept of a Person, and Other Essays*, Macmillan, 1963).
—— *The Origins of Pragmatism* (Macmillan, 1968).
BENNETT, J. F.: 'Real' (*Mind*, 1966).
CODER, D.: 'Some Misconceptions About Dispositions' (*Analysis*, 1969).
CORNMAN, J. W.: 'Strawson's "Person" ' (*Theoria*, 1964).
DESCARTES, R.: *Meditations* (in *Descartes' Philosophical Works*, trans. Haldane and Ross, C.U.P., 1911).
—— *Descartes' Philosophical Writings* (ed. and trans. N. Kemp-Smith, Macmillan, 1952).
FEIGL, H.: 'Mind-Body, Not a Pseudo-Problem' (in S. Hook (ed.): *Dimensions of Mind*, Collier Books, 1961).
—— *The 'Mental' and the 'Physical'* (Minnesota Studies in the Philosophy of Science, Vol. II, Minnesota, 1958; reprinted, with a Postscript, Minnesota, 1967).
FEYERABEND, P.: 'Materialism and the Mind-Body Problem' (*Review of Metaphysics*, 1963–4).
GRICE, H. P.: 'Meaning' (*Philosophical Review*, 1957).
—— 'Personal Identity' (*Mind*, 1941).
—— 'Utterer's Meaning and Intentions' (*Philosophical Review*, 1969).
HART, H. L. A.: 'The Ascription of Responsibility and Rights' (*Proceedings of the Aristotelian Society*, 1948–9).
JAMES, W.: *Principles of Psychology* (Macmillan, 1890).
KANT, I.: *Critique of Pure Reason* (trans. Kemp-Smith, Macmillan, 1929).
KENNY, A. J. P.: *Action, Emotion and Will* (Routledge and Kegan Paul, 1963).
KÖRNER, S.: *Experience and Theory* (Routledge and Kegan Paul, 1966).

LLEWELYN, J. E.: 'The Inconceivability of Pessimistic Determinism' (*Analysis*, 1966).

LOCKE, J.: *Essay Concerning Human Understanding*.

MACKAY, D. M.: 'Towards an Information-Flow Model of Human Behaviour' (*British Journal of Psychology*, 1956).

MALCOLM, N.: 'Anselm's Ontological Arguments' (*Philosophical Review*, 1960).

—— 'Scientific Materialism and the Identity Theory' (abstract in *Journal of Philosophy*, 1963).

—— 'The Conceivability of Mechanism' (*Philosophical Review*, 1968).

MELDEN, A. I.: *Free Action* (Routledge and Kegan Paul, 1961).

PENELHUM, T.: *Survival and Disembodied Existence* (Routledge and Kegan Paul, 1970).

PUCCETTI, R.: 'Brain Transplantation and Personal Identity' (*Analysis*, 1969).

QUINE, W. V. O.: *Word and Object* (M.I.T., 1960).

QUINTON, A. M.: 'The Soul' (*Journal of Philosophy*, 1962).

RAMSEY, F. P.: 'Facts and Propositions' (*Proceedings of the Aristotelian Society*, Supplementary Vol., 1927; reprinted in *Foundations of Mathematics*, Routledge and Kegan Paul, 1931).

RYLE, G.: *The Concept of Mind* (Hutchinson, 1949).

SEARLE, J.: 'Austin on Locutionary and Illocutionary Acts' (*Philosophical Review*, 1968).

—— 'Meaning and Speech-Acts' (*Philosophical Review*, 1962).

—— *Speech-Acts* (C.U.P., 1969).

SELLARS, W.: *Science and Metaphysics* (Routledge and Kegan Paul, 1968).

—— 'Philosophy and the Scientific Image of Man' (in *Science, Perception and Reality*, Routledge and Kegan Paul, 1963).

SHAFFER, J.: 'Persons and their Bodies' (*Philosophical Review*, 1966).

SHOEMAKER, S.: *Self-Knowledge and Self-Identity* (Cornell U.P., 1963).

SMART, J. J. C.: 'Materialism' (*Journal of Philosophy*, 1963).

—— *Philosophy and Scientific Realism* (Routledge and Kegan Paul, 1963).

SOMMERS, F.: 'Types and Ontology' (*Philosophical Review*, 1963).

SQUIRES, J. E. R.: 'Are Dispositions Causes?' (*Analysis*, 1968).

STEVENSON, L.: 'Are Dispositions Causes?' (*Analysis*, 1969).

STRAWSON, P. F.: *The Bounds of Sense* (Methuen, 1966).

—— *Individuals* (Methuen, 1959).

—— 'Intention and Convention in Speech-Acts' (*Philosophical Review*, 1965).

TAYLOR, R.: *Action and Purpose* (Prentice-Hall, 1966).

WILLIAMS, B. A. O.: 'Bodily Identity and Continuity: A Reply' (*Analysis*, 1960).
—— 'Personal Identity and Individuation' (*Proceedings of the Aristotelian Society*, 1956–7).
—— 'The Self and the Future' (*Philosophical Review*, 1970).
WITTGENSTEIN, L.: *Blue and Brown Books* (Basil Blackwell, 1958).
—— *Philosophical Investigations* (Basil Blackwell, 2nd edn., 1958).
—— *Tractatus Logico-Philosophicus* (trans. D. F. Pears and B. F. McGuinness, Routledge and Kegan Paul, 1961).

INDEX